183204

ARMY

The U.S. Army Today

The Great Seal of the United States, adopted in 1782, may be found on many badges, pins, emblems, and devices associated with the Army, including this version from the visored cap worn by male officers.

ARMY

The U.S. Army Today

CHARTWELL
BOOKS, INC.

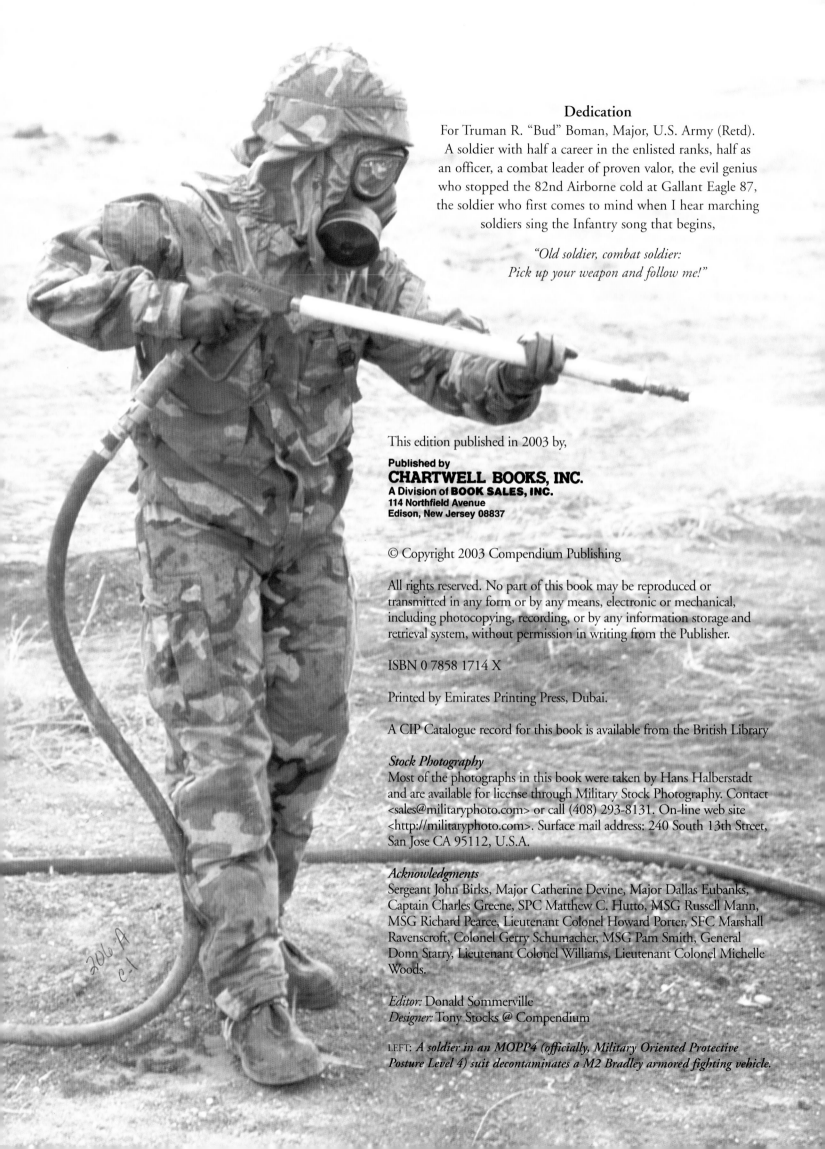

Dedication

For Truman R. "Bud" Boman, Major, U.S. Army (Retd).
A soldier with half a career in the enlisted ranks, half as
an officer, a combat leader of proven valor, the evil genius
who stopped the 82nd Airborne cold at Gallant Eagle 87,
the soldier who first comes to mind when I hear marching
soldiers sing the Infantry song that begins,

"Old soldier, combat soldier:
Pick up your weapon and follow me!"

This edition published in 2003 by,

Published by
CHARTWELL BOOKS, INC.
A Division of BOOK SALES, INC.
114 Northfield Avenue
Edison, New Jersey 08837

ISBN 0 7858 1714 X

Printed by Emirates Printing Press, Dubai.

A CIP Catalogue record for this book is available from the British Library

Stock Photography
Most of the photographs in this book were taken by Hans Halberstadt
and are available for license through Military Stock Photography. Contact
<sales@militaryphoto.com> or call (408) 293-8131. On-line web site
<http://militaryphoto.com>. Surface mail address: 240 South 13th Street,
San Jose CA 95112, U.S.A.

Acknowledgments
Sergeant John Birks, Major Catherine Devine, Major Dallas Eubanks,
Captain Charles Greene, SPC Matthew C. Hutto, MSG Russell Mann,
MSG Richard Pearce, Lieutenant Colonel Howard Porter, SFC Marshall
Ravenscroft, Colonel Gerry Schumacher, MSG Pam Smith, General
Donn Starry, Lieutenant Colonel Williams, Lieutenant Colonel Michelle
Woods.

Editor: Donald Sommerville
Designer: Tony Stocks @ Compendium

LEFT: *A soldier in an MOPP4 (officially, Military Oriented Protective
Posture Level 4) suit decontaminates a M2 Bradley armored fighting vehicle.*

Contents

Preface

There are lots of ways to look at an institution—from the outside in, or inside out, from the top down, or bottom up; you can look at its missions or its missionaries, its tools of the trade, or its tactics. Institutions may be studied historically, looking back, or predictively, toward the future. From any of these viewpoints, the U.S. Army is an interesting, immense topic. Over the years I have had the odd privilege of looking at the Army from all these perspectives, in a way few others of any rank or station are permitted.

Invariably, I have made photographs of soldiers and of soldiering, tens of thousands of photographs of tankers and Rangers and Apache pilots and truck drivers. I've watched Private E-1s get their first haircuts and make their first, feeble hand salutes. I've watched and photographed four-star general officers with 40 years of service come back to inspect their good works.

I've always thought that Americans really didn't know these people very well—who they are, what they do, how they learn their business, how they all fit together. The whole story, of course, is too big to fit neatly into any one book, or even a set of encyclopedias for that matter, so what I have done here is to put together a kind of Army family photo album. As with any family album, some people show up in more photos than others. I've emphasized what the Army calls the "combat arms," the trigger-pullers, over some of the swell people who serve in supporting roles. I've emphasized the enlisted soldier's story here, and the junior officer's story, because that's where the action is. These are the people who do the shooting, and who get shot at. They are my friends, they are my professional descendants, and this book is really about them and their institution today, the modern United States Army.

RIGHT: *"Are we having fun yet?" Observer-Controllers (called OCs) enjoy the sunrise while a bunker complex burns in the background after an artillery prep by M109A6 self propelled howitzers. While they wait, a company of combat engineers are moving into postion for their final assault, breaching a wire barrier, clearing mines, then clearing the bunkers and trenches of the position.*

OPPOSITE, LEFT: *Specialist Jillian Basso, 82nd Airborne Division, has started wearing her makeup a bit differently since joining the Army, but the guys in her unit wear the same foundation and eye-liner, and put it on the same way. This is the standard, approved, pattern for "war paint," used with many variations by all soldiers.*

OPPOSITE, RIGHT: *Chemical warfare became big business after World War II, and more so now. The suits are hot and uncomfortable but all soldiers learn to use them. This team is practicing decontaminating vehicles.*

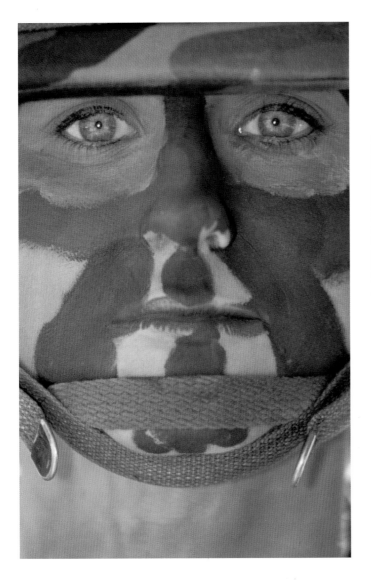

Adventures of a "Strap-Hanger"

There's an old and honorable tradition in the U.S. Army that works something like this: find an ancient old soldier and prop him up someplace with a beer in one wrinkled and trembling hand and then provoke Old Sarge by saying something about the Army of today—the weapons, training, physical fitness, equipment, tactics, or any other aspect of the institution. You are almost guaranteed to get a six-beer, two-hour monologue on the "old Army" and its limitless virtues.

When I enlisted, the World War II vets, when they talked about it at all, referred to the organization as "…the old 'brown-shoe' Army" but today the old Army is the one I joined four decades ago, just as the war in Vietnam was beginning to simmer.

Over the years, I have heard many grizzled graybeards singing the praises of all kinds of features of this ancient and fabled congregation—the accuracy of the 8-inch gun, the superiority of the M14 over the M16, the toughness of soldiers back in the days before …well, it must have been thus since George Washington was a corporal, and probably before.

Through the magic of time, I have somehow become that old soldier, and I am now become that Old Sarge. And although that mythical "brown-shoe" Army was even before my own time, and although almost everything is different now, I am here to testify that today's Army is better than ever—better weapons, training, doctrine, and best of all, better soldiers.

Today's U.S. Army is a wonderfully healthy, and mostly happy, institution, better in *almost* every way. It has, over the past few decades, re-designed itself tremendously successfully. I have been watching this process, as the tactics, training, weapons, doctrine, communications, and the individuals of this grand assembly have all evolved and been tested in training and in battle. It has been a great pleasure and privilege but one that few Americans outside the Army are allowed to share.

My perspective on all this is quite unusual, for better and worse. Unlike nearly any commentator on any aspect of the modern armed forces, I am not a retired officer, or former "Green Beret," or Hoover Institution academic or CNN reporter. I'm just a guy who joined the Army, got a little combat time in Vietnam, and then—pretty much by accident—was hired to write books about various communities within the U.S. Department of Defense.

The result has been an odd odyssey that has had me "embedded" with dozens of units of all the armed forces, sometimes for quite extended periods. Soldiers call such alien visitors, and there are many, "strap-hangers," an expression that identifies somebody along for the ride but not really in the chain of command. Such a role provides the opportunity for tremendous insights into a community and I have had the chance to evaluate dozens of units—Army, Navy, Air Force, Marine Corps, and Coast Guard, along with small units of the British Army and Russian Air Force—from the inside. It is sometimes quite revealing, and not always in a flattering way. That's because, once you have been around for a day or two, and as long as you don't cause trouble, a strap-hanger fairly quickly becomes part of the environment. Some soldiers will ooze up to you, not quite sure what to say, and ask, "Ah, sir …who ARE you, anyway?" As long as you can convince these people that you're not from a congressional investigation of some sort, they tend to be very hospitable.

But not always. It is curious how different Army companies and battalions each have their own "personality," but they do, and some are better than others. Some are composed of nothing but brilliant, funny, hard-charging, evangelical, hard-core, troopers—120 of them, all in one place at one time. You can go across the street, hang out with another company in another battalion, and find a company of 120 sullen, lazy, whining, slovenly, losers. While I have spent time with both kinds of units, nearly all have been the former—starting with Lieutenant Colonel (LTC) Gerry Schumacher's 3rd Battalion, 12th Special Forces, or LTC Tim Wray's 3rd Battalion, 17th Infantry Regiment, 7th Infantry Division, LTC Rick Riera's 2nd Battalion, 8th Infantry Regiment, 4th Infantry Division, and many others.

The foundation for these successful, happy units turn out to be successful, happy commanders. When the commander is confident in himself and his subordinates, the feeling somehow infects the whole unit and helps it accomplish great things. He manages to surround himself with successful staff officers and NCOs, each of whom is confident and competent at his specialty, and the whole process works up and down the organization, right down to the PFCs and fire team leaders. Being in the company of such units is a great pleasure, even for alien observers. This book is based on many of them.

Acknowledgments
Sergeant John Birks, Major Catherine Devine, Major Dallas Eubanks, Captain Charles Greene, SPC Matthew C. Hutto, MSG Russell Mann, MSG Richard Pearce, Lieutenant Colonel Howard Porter, SFC Marshall Ravenscroft, Colonel Gerry Schumacher, MSG Pam Smith, General Donn Starry, Lieutenant Colonel Williams, Lieutenant Colonel Michelle Woods.

RIGHT: *The Army's old love affair with the jeep continues with HMWWVs, or "humvees," a bigger, sturdier, more comfortable go-anywhere vehicle owned by virtually every combat unit. They come in many variations but many are loaded with radios and serve as the commander's home away from home. In the back of every one of these will be 5-gallon water cans, cases of MREs, rucksacks, and about ten pounds of dust and dirt mixed in with everything else.*

Introduction

A Brief History of An Evolving Institution

Military units are very much like families, and, like families, there is always a little friction within them, a lot of jobs to be done, and a kind of clannish identity. Also, like families, there is always an evolutionary process at work. For the Army, it is pretty easy to identify "generations" or stages—the World War II vets had one view of their Army, the Korean and Cold War era soldiers another, my own Vietnam vets yet another, and the soldiers of today a sense of community that is utterly unlike that of any previous era.

Although this is a book about the modern Army, it is so different from the Army of the past that a bit of background may help the reader appreciate it all. Forty years ago, the U.S. Army was composed of a mixed bag of World War II career soldiers getting ready to retire, a large number of

sullen draftees on two-year or six-month active duty, plus a few "Regulars" who enlisted for a three-year period.

Dodging the Draft

All American males had, until the mid-1970s, a six-year military obligation. Draftees who had the foresight to join a Guard or Reserve unit before hearing from their draft board served only six months on active duty, two months of which was Basic Training, another month or two of Advanced Individual Training, followed by another couple of months goofing off and getting in the way. Then it was back home and a routine of one weekend a month with the Reserve or Guard unit plus two weeks of annual summer camp. Draftees who were not already attached to a unit served two years, then went back to civil life without monthly drills or

summer camp, but always subject to recall if warm bodies were required.

The draft had some great advantages for the Army and for America, and some major downsides, too. It provided a huge pool of men who were at least slightly familiar with military discipline, could tell one end of a rifle from another, and had a kind of kindergarten-level set of skills that could be put to use if and when—as the expression for the outset of World War III was at the time—"the balloon went up." During the draft era, almost every American male had at least some experience with the armed forces, and virtually all American families knew men who were in one of the services. The result was a very democratic institution, a place where men from all classes, all colors (after integration), and all educational backgrounds got to know each other, work together, and live together—for better as well as worse.

The draft was good in many ways for America, and for most Americans, but it was lousy for the Army. The draftees who had obtained deferments to attend college, for example, were older, wiser, weaker, and utterly unmotivated. They did the very minimum required to keep out of trouble—if that. They were often malcontents, hostile,

argumentative. One of the fundamental requirements of the time for any sergeant, especially a basic training sergeant, was the ability to go one-on-one with any man in his unit, out behind the barracks. Maintaining discipline through physical violence was, of course, prohibited by regulations, but unless a trainee was killed or seriously injured, I doubt that the regulation was often enforced.

Every basic training company included some men, sometimes draftees, sometimes enlistees, who were of very low intelligence and very poorly educated. Draft boards made it possible for just about every young man to serve his country, including some who were nearly illiterate. While these balanced the Ph.D.s pretty well, and insured that the Army got men from all walks of life, it made unit cohesion weak.

RA All the Way!

Mixed in with the draftees were the Regulars, a term that was once a mark of pride and that is now unknown. An enlistee signed up for three years active duty, was offered an opportunity to chose what kind of advanced training he wanted (although his actual assignment might be different), and had a three-year Reserve obligation after discharge, although the chance of being assigned to a drilling unit was, for Regulars, remote. A Regular's service number began with the letters RA (mine was RA19726738), and for most was a little beacon of pride. While some Regulars enlisted just to get their obligation over with, others were attracted by the idea of military service. With World War II successfully and honorably concluded by our fathers, some of us wanted to share the experience—despite what our fathers might have had to say by way of warning.

Regulars tended to be younger than the draftees, in better physical condition, with fewer bad habits, fewer attitude problems, and were actually anxious to be good soldiers.

Combining these bright-eyed young acolytes with the grumpy, older, wiser malcontents was asking for trouble. But worse was yet to come.

End of the Draft

The U.S. Army started sending soldiers to Vietnam and Southeast Asia in the late 1950s and kept soldiers fighting there till 1973. The quality of the soldiers deteriorated steadily, with increasing friction between the gung-ho Regulars and career NCOs against the draftees. In the end President Nixon finally abolished the draft and the Army converted quickly to an all-volunteer force. If anything, the initial result was even worse.

For a variety of reasons, the Army of the mid-1970s found itself enlisting some of the worst excuses for soldiers since the Civil War—the very dregs of society, with a large criminal class. Officers considered themselves fortunate to get an occasional salute, and attempts to discipline many junior enlisted soldiers of this era frequently provoked physical assaults. It was not a happy time for the Army, and many long-serving and dedicated officers and NCOs resigned in disgust.

But then a wonderful thing, from the Army's point of view, happened—a major recession. The unemployment rate went through the roof. Highly educated, intelligent, and law-abiding young men and women suddenly found themselves out of work, and likely to remain so, unless they wanted to sign up for a few years in the Army. It was the answer to a recruiter's prayer. These Army recruiters found a line out the door of college graduates, young people with self-discipline, self-esteem, and ambition. The high-school drop-outs and criminal class were no longer welcome at the recruiting office, and the ones who had already enlisted soon found themselves back in civilian clothes with Bad Conduct discharges. Quite rapidly the Army was full of sharp, energetic, ambitious team-players. The ranks once again contained college graduates, but unlike those of the draft era, these were here because they wanted to be. This sudden infusion of new blood invigorated the Army, gave it a new sense of power and purpose. But, for the most part, the American public didn't notice or care.

The Cloistered Army

The end of the draft changed the flow of people into the Army and then the Army changed the way it kept them in uniform. Instead of a huge flow of people rotating quickly in and out of the enlisted ranks, the Army started working to keep individuals serving longer. Pay was improved, the quality of people within units was improved, and the turmoil of the draft years ended. Huge percentages of first-hitch enlistees re-enlisted ("re-upped" is the vernacular expression); the Army didn't have continually to train people for the same jobs at the previous frantic rate—these soldiers and their skills stayed and grew, and this improved both the soldiers and their units.

No longer were America's aristocratic families and criminal families the only ones sending their boys off to serve as Regulars. Now the Army was becoming very middle class, with few of the social extremes. The recession abated and the job market improved, but a lot of the soldiers who joined because they had few choices decided to stay after that first enlistment. All the old soldiers noticed the difference in the ranks—soldiers were smarter, more independent, and had to be led in somewhat different ways if NCOs and officers were to earn their respect.

As the Army of the 1970s and 80s became more professional, it also became more cloistered. Without the rapid turnover in the ranks, fewer and fewer Americans were serving, or even knew anyone serving. The Army was re-inventing itself, and nobody noticed.

One of the reasons the vast American public didn't notice what was happening was that the Army was old news. With the Vietnam War over in seeming disgrace, newspapers and television news operations seldom paid any attention, except perhaps to produce hit pieces and hatchet jobs like the San Jose, California, *Mercury-News'* series on the supposed faults and flaws of the then-new M-2 Bradley armoured fighting vehicle. The anti-war movement was also an anti-military movement and feelings in the nation were still strongly hostile to the Army and other services.

So there was a mutual antipathy between the Army and the people who reported on the Army. The walls went up, the gates closed, and the new, professional Army became something of a monastic order, a place where people who had a calling adopted a new way of life, a new kind of language, world view, clothing, and mission, far from the distractions of civil life. When the Army went to war, first in Grenada, then in Panama, and then in the Gulf, it was without the hordes of photographers and reporters who had covered Vietnam. The news media were kept at a distance, and the soldiers and their commanders liked it that way. They especially liked the way the same news organizations that had been so critical of soldiers and soldiering now howled in protest at being excluded.

RIGHT: *Soldiers, more than other Americans, understand and confront risk and danger and fear. Many of them, men and women both, volunteer for the Basic Airborne Course and learn how to jump out of perfectly good aircraft in a military manner. Military parachuting has very little in common with sport parachuting – it is a way to deliver people to combat zones, in large numbers or small, in daylight or the darkest night, with weapons and equipment with which to fight on arrival. This is a user's view of the beautiful T-10 canopy, the basic design of which has been in use for sixty years.*

Battle of the Sexes

Among the revolutionary changes for the Army and all the other armed forces was a congressionally mandated new policy on the role of women. Before 1978, women in the Army were members of the Women's Army Corps (WAC) and were restricted largely to clerical functions. Beginning in the late 1970s women began to be integrated into most of the military occupational specialties (MOSs) performed by men. Women were allowed to go to the Basic Airborne Course ("Jump School"), work as vehicle mechanics, fly helicopters, drive trucks and heavy equipment, and all sorts of other activities previously considered unladylike.

Predictably, this new policy created an uproar, with predictions of the end of the world by some, and predictions of a new, much more capable, Army by others. There were loud forecasts that the Army would be tremendously improved by having women in the ranks of nearly all units (only direct combat units excepted). On the other side were equally loud predictions of orgies, fraternization, lowered physical fitness standards, and all imaginable kinds of "female trouble."

It has been a quarter century since the policy changed, and both sets of predictions have turned out to come true—in part. Women now comprise about ten percent of the whole Army and are found almost everywhere. Many of them are outstanding soldiers, NCOs, and officers, just as predicted. They get along well with their male counterparts, pull their weight, and don't fall out during PT.

At the same time, though, the people who predicted that putting men and women together, far from home and family, under stress, in sometimes exciting and romantic environments would have them all breeding like rabbits were also correct. There is a lot of sexual activity in the barracks, in the field, and on deployments—no matter what anybody tries to tell you. It is one of the informal secrets of the armed forces, and still a major unresolved issue with dangerous operational implications that nobody wants to discuss. When the Army and other services deployed to the Gulf in 1990 and 1991, the primary cause for evacuation from the combat zone was pregnancy.

Another issue for the traditionalists was the likelihood of lowered physical fitness standards and, to a certain extent, this prediction has also come true. It seems reasonable enough that there are different standards for men and women, as well as for different age groups, but the differences are extreme: a 20-year-old male ROTC cadet must do 43 correct push-ups to meet the minimum standard or he is rejected from the program. A female cadet's standard is 17. Both male and female students at the Basic Airborne Course are now permitted to have someone "boost" them—assist from behind by giving them a lift—while doing pull-ups, a nod, the "Black Hats" say, to keeping the numbers of women in the school up.

The process of figuring out exactly the best way to integrate women in the Army is still evolving, but it has largely been a success. Women who meet the standard, become part of a unit and execute their duties in a professional way are highly regarded. The others are weeded out—but so are the men who don't quite fit.

Hoo-ah, FIDO, Good To Go and the Secret Language of Soldiers

One of the things that happens when people become members of exotic religious and civil orders is that they develop their own specialized language, rituals, sense of humor, and traditions. In the years since the conversion to an all-volunteer Army, this evolution has been going full blast, with new terms, expressions, and ceremonies becoming part of the institution, utterly out of sight of the civilian world.

The first such example I noticed was the phrase "good to go," something I first heard in the 82nd Airborne back about 1985. This expression might have been in use before that, but I certainly didn't encounter it. Good to go means that you are ready for whatever the current mission is—and that can be anything from a parachute jump into enemy territory to being all dressed up for a big date. When the jumpmaster finishes inspecting you and your gear (officially, a "jumpmaster

LEFT AND FAR LEFT: *The Army, and the Marine Corps, too, have an almost religious commitment to the importance of groups of people working together as teams focused on a particular mission. – whether that mission is combat infantry or resupply. The individuals in these teams – the squads, platoons, companies, battalions – are in constant transition, with missions in frequent flux, but a big part of soldiering involves working effectively with people, communication skills, and management decisions. Soldiers learn to lead and follow and put mission before self, unto death if required.*

personnel inspection," but always referred to as being "J-M-P-Ied"), he swats you on the butt and says, "You're good to go." Good to go has infiltrated civilian American slang, but is an exception in that respect.

FIDO is another recent addition to the lexicon of American slang. It abbreviates, "f*** it, drive on," and is a way of indicating that the obstacle that you are whining about should not prevent you from getting on with the business at hand. High-speed/low-drag used to be a common expression but seems to have mostly disappeared. It referred to any tool, weapon, object, idea, person, or tactic that was in some way excellent. A sharp soldier might be described as high-speed/low-drag, but so might a knife, radio, actress, automobile, or all sorts of other objects, but never intangibles—though these can be good-to-go.

Currently, the operative secret slogan is "hoo-ah." Although this expression is supposed to go back to the Seminole Wars, I certainly didn't start to hear it till about five years ago. The Army is trying to use hoo-ah in recruiting, much to the confusion of civilians and old soldiers. Hoo-ah is used to mean almost anything, almost anytime, and I bet that at the conclusion of sermons in all the little chapels on Fort Bragg, the congregation doesn't say "amen," they proclaim "Hoo-AH!" instead.

These and many more words and expressions comprise a large, witty, and private vocabulary that is in constant development and transition. Words and phrases come and go.

Some units, some occupational specialties, have their own, even more private, lexicon. It is all part of the rich sub-culture of the Army and its people.

Challenge Coins and the "I Love Me" Wall

Another development of the new volunteer Army is the new tradition of the challenge coin. This tradition is supposed to have originated in the Special Forces community during the Vietnam War, but had pretty well migrated to the rest of the Army by the late 1980s when I got my first coin from the 7th Infantry Division (Light). Not having encountered the tradition previously, this was perplexing. My friend, a "staff weenie" public affairs officer, presented me with a large coin upon which was engraved my name. The coin was also embossed with the division's trademark spider and spider-web. I was honored without quite knowing why.

The explanation was that all kinds of units had by then decided to produce a coin of their own, normally presented to people as a kind of tangible "thank-you." First sergeants carry a supply of these around in their BDUs and hand them out to anybody who has done something good. It is difficult to be in or around the Army very long without accumulating a supply of these things, which would be great, except for one thing—you've got to carry one of them with you at all times and selecting the one can be a problem. The problem is that there is more to the tradition than just having the coin. At any moment of any day, and especially in bars frequented by soldiers, any drunk can holler, "Coin check!" You then have thirty seconds to produce your coin or buy a round of drinks for the bar.

Displays of challenge coins are a standard feature of another requirement for today's soldier, the "I love me" wall. All soldiers over the rank of E-6 are required by modern tradition to have and maintain at home or office a wall decorated with photographs, certificates, framed guidons, and similar mementos—often including dozens of unit coins. A whole cottage industry has developed to service this tradition, and especially in Korea or around major installations like Fort Bragg or Fort Hood, will be found shops producing custom-made military awards, all of which are destined for somebody's "I love me" wall. So, if you start getting coins, make room for them in your display—but be sure to keep one in your wallet if you ever go to bars.

CHAPTER 1 Training and Qualifications

CHAPTER 1 Training and Qualifications

Soldiers spend a tremendous amount of time in formal training classes and programs, especially at the early stages of their careers. And for those who go on to more responsible roles in the NCO and commissioned officer ranks, there will be highly challenging courses that will determine who wears the insignia of a Command Sergeant Major (CSM) or general officer.

Entry Level Training

Every soldier goes through a variation on the same military ordeal. For those joining the enlisted ranks, it begins with a nine-week (currently) Basic Training course. Men and women who intend to become officers have several possible paths—the U.S. Military Academy at West Point (USMA), the Reserve Officer Training Course (ROTC) in conjunction

with work toward a Batchelor's degree at many four-year universities, Officer Candidate School (OCS) for enlisted soldiers, Warrant Officer programs for certain soldiers with very specialized skills, particularly in aviation, and finally, direct commission for some with very advanced professional skills, including physicians and chaplains. Everybody except the direct commission officers goes through the same fundamentals, but the officer candidates are held to a much higher standard on everything and go through a much longer program.

Basic

Current Army Basic Training lasts nine weeks and provides a foundation for every modern soldier. The program changes frequently in small ways, but some things never change. New

RIGHT: *Well, we have a long way to go with this guy. Day One in Basic Training, and the recruits are fresh off the bus, waiting for The Haircut. While they are waiting, a sergeant takes the opportunity to teach them the position of attention and the hand salute. He'll learn to do it correctly soon enough, or suffer the consequences, normally a bit of undivided, close up attention from the drill instructor and perhaps a few pushups.*

PREVIOUS PAGE: *The Army has always had its ways for getting the attention of wayward soldiers, and the Gig Pit at Jump School used to be one, recently abolished. These soldiers have been placed in the position called "front leaning rest," and they have been this way for a while. "You can stay there till I get tired!" one of the Black Hats has probably said, and he doesn't tire in any position. Physical fitness is one part of soldiering, and doing what you are told, promptly, is another, as these soldiers are discovering the hard way.*

LEFT: *When basic trainees are not running a course or listening to instruction, they are expected to be studying. The amount of knowledge – of general orders, chain of command, weapons systems, first aid procedures, and much more – that each trainee must absorb and understand and repeat is huge. Few college students work so hard at scholarship.*

BELOW LEFT: *What's this guy smiling about? Well, Goldilocks is finally getting shorn and the job is half way done. Very short hair is fashionable in the Army, but it hasn't always been so. Until soldiers finish Basic, haircuts are almost to the skin – later, a modified version called "high and tight" is acceptable and popular.*

enlistees report to one of about five installations and begin Week Zero, where miracles begin to happen. The recruit has, up till now, been accustomed to the sergeant-recruiter as his good friend and advisor who has, in a gentle and kindly way, explained the many joys of the Army, and how much fun Basic Training will be. Once the trainee has signed the contract, sworn the oath, and reported to the induction station, the party is over.

Basic Training NCOs are wonderful soldiers—once you get to know them. I remember mine, Sergeant Green, quite well. Every soldier remembers his or her platoon NCO at least as well as his or her mother, and sometimes with more affection. That's because your basic training sergeant is rather like your mother, only more effective. Much more effective. Mothers spend approximately 18 years trying to get their offspring to stand up straight, clean their room, have polite manners, and keep themselves clean and tidy, all with normally quite limited success.

An Army drill instructor, however, will accomplish all this and more, and do it in about 18 minutes instead of 18 years. Very few trainees talk back to their NCOs, or slouch, or fail to shower or brush their teeth. They keep their living spaces spotless, their shoes shined to a high luster, and instead of replying "Huh?" when asked a simple question, quickly learn to respond "YES, SERGEANT!" or "NO, SERGEANT!" Basic trainees learn to pay attention, do what they are told instantly, refrain from needless questions, and to suffer in silence. At the end of the nine weeks, when mothers finally get to inspect their babies again, the transformation brings a tear to many a maternal eye.

The nine weeks provide each new soldier with a very rudimentary introduction to the use of weapons, especially the M16A2 rifle, with which most become somewhat proficient. Trainees learn to march, learn a little bit about patrolling, a little about tear gas, a little about physical fitness, and a lot about themselves. Even in order to begin, each recruit has to pass a three-part physical fitness test that involves push-ups, sit-ups, and a run, with different standards for men and women. Men in the 17–21 age category, for example, have to do 43 push-ups (back straight, full extension of the arms, then all the way down till the chest touches the ground); women in the same age category have to do 17. Men have to do at least 58 sit-ups, women 36. Men get 19 minutes, 30 seconds to run two miles while the women get three additional minutes to complete the distance.

The current Basic Training program has three phases. First comes several weeks of fundamentals that teach the individual recruit about marching, General Orders, the ranks from Private E-1 to General O-10. There is a lot of PT, a lot of book work and classroom study, presentations on sexual harassment, and anatomy lessons on the M16A2 rifle.

Phase II continues much of the training of the previous weeks but now emphasizes proficiency with weapons. Trainees learn to shoot, beginning at 50-foot targets where they "zero" their weapons, followed by many days on the longer ranges firing at pop-up targets that appear and disappear at random, at distances from 25 meters to 300 meters. All trainees get some bayonet training (although it is very unlikely that they will ever use it) and throw inert, then live, M67 fragmentation grenades. They run an assault course, over and over. At the end of Phase II, each fires for qualification and many earn their first decoration—a Marksman, Sharpshooter, or Expert Rifleman badge.

Phase III takes individuals and puts them to work in teams. The novice soldiers learn patrol skills, movement techniques, and cooperation. At the end of this phase, after eight weeks of intensive training and nearly at the end of Basic Training, comes a final, culminating ordeal, an event the Army calls Victory Forge. Based on the Marine Corps' even more demanding Crucible test, Victory Forge pushes trainees day and night with little food or sleep through a series of events that require teamwork, initiative, stamina, and strength. Currently, this is a three-day event with two road marches, one 10km, the other 15km, a night infiltration course, and other competitions.

At the end of Victory Forge, the sleepy, hungry, tired— and elated—young trainees are pushed up one last hill or double-time one last mile, and are no longer recruits but finally soldiers. For some, it is the most important accomplishment of a lifetime, for others just the beginning of many more, and far more challenging, Army schools.

Advanced Individual Training

Every enlisted soldier goes through the same Basic but after those first nine weeks, things get interesting in a new way. Every soldier has a MOS, or Military Occupational Specialty, and each MOS requires advanced training. Directly after Basic, each soldier is sent to Advanced Individual Training or AIT.

LEFT: *Recruits typically arrive for Basic with poor, sometimes awful, upper body strength. To build them up, a lot of time of each day involves PT or physical training, sometimes with rifles, as here, but more often by doing pushups – hundreds every day, tens of thousands during Basic Training.*

BELOW LEFT: *"Faster! Move! What are you waiting for, private?" The gap is not really that great, but if you've already run a few hundred meters and had to deal with other obstacles, you have to put a little extra horsepower into this one, or fall in the pit. It's painful, and embarrassing, but part of the program.*

Each specialty has its own title and numerical designator. All infantry soldiers have an 11-series MOS, with a basic "leg" rifleman designated an 11B, or "Eleven Bravo." Riflemen trained for mechanized infantry—the guys who get a taxi-ride to the battlefield in an M2 Bradley AFV—have an MOS of 11M, and are referred to as "Eleven Mikes." Special Forces soldiers are in the 18-series, artillerymen are 13s, and so forth.

AIT builds on the basic soldier skills but with more intensity. The infantry soldiers get much more time on the range, in the field, and become proficient at patrolling. The armor soldiers will go off to Fort Knox and learn all there is to know about the Abrams, Bradley, M113, and all the other tracked armored combat vehicles. New artillerymen go to Fort Sill, Oklahoma, and study all the Army's crew-served cannon and rockets. There are schools for cooks, clerks, medics, truck-drivers, helicopter mechanics, helicopter pilots, engineers, signal technicians, interrogators, and even "Green Berets," a recent change in policy. AIT is always changing, based on lessons learned in and out of combat, and generally for the better.

Ring-Knockers, "Rotcees," and Mustangs — The Officer Class

There are, of course, two major classes within the Army, the commissioned officers and the enlisted (or, as the expression once was, "common") soldier. Every commissioned officer holds office at the pleasure of the President of the United States, and with that office comes great responsibilities and great privileges. On paper, at least, the newest and least experienced "Lt. Fuzz" is the social superior of the oldest and wisest sergeant. Old Sarge will always say "sir" to this novice officer—a "butter bar" in the vernacular of the Army, because of the gold color of the entry-level officer's insignia—and will treat him or her with superficial deference, despite a vast gulf in experience. But this is right and proper—even the most baby-faced new officer carries a potential responsibility for the lives and fortunes of his soldiers that even the most senior NCO does not. The "sir" or "ma'am" is a reminder of that role, for both of them. But it is a very foolish new officer indeed who does not listen carefully to the advice of his sergeants, and a rare one, too. West Point, ROTC, and OCS are all a form of basic training for new commissioned officers, but they learn to be effective administrators and leaders when wise old enlisted sergeants—along, of course, with wise old officers—coach them properly.

There are three normal paths to a commission for any young man or woman with an interest in becoming an Army officer, and two alternate ways for people with very specialized skills. While the U.S. Military Academy at West Point is certainly the most famous of these, and has been minting "butter bars" since the 1830s, the Reserve Officer Training Course churns out the vast majority of Army officers, accounting for around 70 percent of the annual total. Officer Candidate School produces the fewest and some of the best. Besides these standard paths to a "butter bar," two other commission options are available, the warrant officer program and direct commission.

LEFT: *"Yes, sergeant!" the trainees respond to a question. "I can't hear you! LOUDER!" "YES, SERGEANT!!" they roar at the top of their voices.*

BELOW LEFT: *Drill instructors are wonderful creatures, and most soldiers recall (some with fondness) the ones who trained them for the rest of their lives. A DI can accomplish in a few days everything a mother tried and failed to do for eighteen years — produce a young man who can stand up straight, cleans his room, is always polite, and does what he is told.*

OPPOSITE, LEFT: *American soldiers can be short or tall, as these two ROTC cadets demonstrate. The woman on the left is well under five feet tall, the man over six, and both are training to become officers.*

OPPOSITE, RIGHT: *New recruits attend Basic Training at several installations around the US, these at Fort Benning, Georgia, home of the infantry. The process takes about nine weeks and gradually prepares the individual to be an entry-level soldier at the most fundamental level — think of it as kindergarten with guns and knives.*

NEXT PAGE: *Turning weak, self-centered, immature civilians into soldiers is an art form many thousands of years old, and some of the techniques used hundreds of years ago are still employed today. These Basic Training recruits are learning all sorts of things at the same time — the most important of which is to do exactly what they are told, immediately, and with enthusiasm.*

Warrant officers hold a commission and are addressed as "sir" or "ma'am" by the enlisted soldiers, but seem to fit somewhere between the two worlds. Warrants are usually very highly trained specialists who do one thing and one thing only for a whole career. Most Army helicopter pilots are warrant officers and will do nothing but fly until they retire. An officer holding a regular commission may also be qualified to fly, but won't do it for long before going off to administrative and command duties. A captain, never a warrant officer, will command a helicopter company.

For some very specialized skills, the Army offers a direct commission without all the stress and strain of the normal programs. The catch, of course, is that you need already to be a fully-fledged physician, a dentist, or a priest. The Army's chaplains and surgeons are required to do very few push-ups before getting their bars—and captain's bars for many of them. To their credit, however, some of these direct-commission officers do PT with the soldiers, go to the field like everybody else, and "hump a ruck" (as the saying goes for anybody who pulls their weight in a unit) like a trooper. The best of these deserve their salutes as much as any officer.

Officer Candidate School

Officer Candidate School is one of the ways the Army manufactures its leaders and, as with graduates of West Point and the ROTC, the officers produced by OCS have their own special qualities and reputation. This program produces the fewest new lieutenants, less than a thousand during recent years, but some of the best prepared for small unit leadership. As Major "Bud" Boman says: "A soldier can't get anything past an OCS officer—he's already seen and done it all and won't put up with the excuses that work with ROTC or USMA graduates."

OCS is a program primarily for enlisted soldiers with college degrees (of whom there are a large number today). While West Point and ROTC spend four years developing their candidates, OCS crams the whole process into 14 thrill-packed weeks and three phases. Besides a high score on the Army's IQ test, a candidate for OCS has to do exceptionally well on the PT test, either have a bachelor's degree or most of the credits required to obtain one, a proven ability to lead soldiers, and be a glutton for punishment. This final requirement isn't official but understood; OCS crams four year's worth of suffering and performance into about 12 weeks.

Basic Phase is like the first phase of Basic Training only much worse. Discipline and PT are much more demanding, with candidates being pushed and stressed constantly. PT is conducted twice every day, and scores on the AFPFT (Armed Forces Physical Fitness Test) are much higher. OCS candidates who arrive from units that don't do much PT are in for a sad surprise.

Survivors move on to Intermediate Phase after four weeks. During the next six weeks OCS candidates spend a lot of time in the field working on infantry fundamentals—patrolling, small unit tactics, command and control of squads, platoons, and companies. Leadership responsibilities rotate constantly, permitting each candidate to succeed or fail in all kinds of officer's roles. All of them get the chance to "command" the student company for a day at a time, and when, for example, the commander makes a mistake during a formation (or any event), one of the instructors is likely to roar, "You're fired! Get back in ranks! XO, take over the company!" There isn't a lot of spare time in 14 weeks for slow learners, or for gentle correction; candidates either absorb it all and perform, or they go back to the enlisted soldier world. A lot of them fail during Phase Two.

But after ten or eleven weeks of this pressure, the remaining candidates graduate to the Advanced Phase and can start to look forward to graduation in another four weeks. First, however, they must successfully absorb vast quantities of information about the administrative functions of an Army officer—a detailed understanding of logistics, military justice, drill and ceremony, administration, and all the rest. At last they begin to feel like officers, and are treated as such by the candidates in Phases One and Two. After about three months of very intense physical and mental pressure the successful candidates pin on the gold bars of a second lieutenant, then attend the Officer Basic Course for their individual branch.

OCS graduates have a good reputation among enlisted soldiers and gain an extra measure of respect even over USMA grads. That's because each OCS graduate (or Mustang according to the traditional nickname for officers who have risen from the enlisted ranks) understands the role of the enlisted man or woman from the perspective of someone who has worn stripes. ROTC and USMA both simulate that experience without actually imposing the enlisted soldier's experience. That's why some captains and majors with 20 years in the Army, half of them as an enlisted

RIGHT: *Only a thousand or so officers are graduated from OCS each year, a program one career officer called "…the best kept secret in the Army." Those accepted already know a great deal about soldiering and have been leading others for year. The stress level is high by design but the actual information imparted tends to be old news for most candidates.*

NEXT PAGE: *The Reserve Officer Training Corps (ROTC) goes back to World War II and allows college students to earn a commission while completing a normal four-year degree program. Sometime during the last two summers, each candidate attends ROTC Advanced Camp at Fort Lewis, Washington, where it all comes together in six weeks of intense training, field problems, leadership exercises, and much drill and ceremony.*

soldier, get an extra measure of respect and an extra crisp salute from the sergeants and the privates.

Reserve Officer Training Course

More than 200 colleges and universities offer the Reserve Officer Training Course, or ROTC. This program is certainly the most productive source of new officers for the Army, accounting for about three out of every four new commissions, and it produces officers in a rather different way than the other programs. An ROTC cadet trains to become an officer while working on a four-year degree and isn't commissioned until the degree is awarded. It is a system that has a reputation for producing well-rounded officers with a sometimes wider world view, and for generating new lieutenants who are intellectually disciplined and who don't always need to be told what to do and how to do it. While OCS and West Point have full-time cadre breathing down the necks of aspiring officers, the ROTC student is more of a self-starter, with a particular brand of initiative not tolerated elsewhere.

Cadets have to meet the same PT standards required of other cadets, but they often train to meet those standards on their own time and alone. Some schools push their cadets harder than others, and the ones with high standards produce graduates that have no trouble at all with the test or with the business of being an Army leader. Many ROTC graduates have made excellent leaders and gone on to wear

stars, General Colin Powell being only one of a large number of examples.

There are three major parts to Army ROTC. First comes two years of course work in "military science," primarily classroom work while the student works toward a bachelor's degree. At the end of this period, qualified students may sign up for two additional years' classroom work, a bit of low-stress PT, and some gentle drill and ceremony. All ROTC cadets in the advanced portion get a stipend and some get scholarships. All must attend Advanced Camp during the summer following either their third or fourth year. After successfully completing the coursework and Advanced Camp, a cadet is commissioned as a second lieutenant in the U.S. Army.

The big test comes at Advanced Camp, a three-week experience that is somewhat stressful for some of the cadets but that OCS and USMA officer candidates would consider a vacation. Fort Lewis, Washington, hosts Advanced Camp every year. Cadets get medical exams and inoculations and are assigned to cadet companies. They are housed in World War II barracks, nearly the last examples of this very spartan form of architecture. One of the very first events at Advanced Camp is the PT test, and a failure here results in a ticket home for many aspiring officers. As with the rest of the Army, there are two sets of standards, one for the men, another for the women, and a lot of men are failed for scores on the push-up portion of the test that would rate a 100-point score for the women.

LEFT: *Cadet Suzanne Johnson comes from a good Army family, with a Ranger brother to lead the way. She participated in ROTC in high school, was selected Battalion Commander of the ROTC unit at her home school, Michigan State, in her senior year, and was commissioned in June, 2002.*

BELOW LEFT: *Physical performance standards for cadet men and women are quite different, with most female cadets getting a GO with seventeen or better pushups while male cadets are required to do forty three minimum. This woman is doing hers to specification – back perfectly straight, hands shoulder-width apart; now, all the way down, and all the way back up to full extension, elbows locked, makes one repetition. Each cadet is tested individually and quite a few fail – but not this woman.*

FAR LEFT: *Cadet Ross has already earned the coveted Air Assault badge, a considerable challenge. Others attend the Basic Airborne Course and wear paratrooper wings on their BDUs even before going to Advanced Camp, both important accomplishments that demand a fair amount of physical strength and mental determination.*

Preparation for the PT test varies from school to school, with some sending cadets poorly prepared, others ready to knock out the push-ups (43 for the men, 17 for the women), the sit-ups, and two-mile run. Failure on the first day results in a chance to re-test on the next.

Advanced Camp introduces cadets to the Leadership Reaction Course, the Obstacle Course, advanced patrolling, firing the M16 for record, and occasional road marches. Each of the 17 Army branches—infantry, armor, adjutant general, transportation, aviation, Special Forces, and the rest—makes a pitch to try to convince each candidate to select their specialty. Some of these branches are, everybody knows, not very glamorous, so these presentations can become quite theatrical. The presenter for the Nuclear, Biological, Chemical (NBC) officer specialty begins by asking the cadets: "Okay, cadets, what do the letters 'NBC' stand for?" The cadets (who have been primed for this) yell back in unison: "NO BODY CARES!" "That's right," he says, "but YOU should care because… " and goes on to make his sales pitch.

They all get a little taste of the Army at its cleanest and best. They march up to a range where an M198 howitzer demonstrates a TOT, or time-on-target artillery mission, first firing one massive shell on a high trajectory, then quickly being reloaded and fired again, on command. The cadets see both rounds detonate simultaneously over a target downrange. Then they spend the rest of the morning being taught the fundamentals of artillery by NCOs who do this show every year.

LEFT: *Cadet Gibbs consults with one of the many cadre that train and lead the leaders of the future. She is, at the moment this photograph was made, brigade commander, a position that is assigned to many candidates during the Advanced Camp experience.*

FAR LEFT: *Each of these ROTC cadets will have opportunities to lead and to follow, and will make plenty of mistakes doing both. A tremendous amount of information is presented during Advanced Camp, but it isn't really an academic experience. Instead, these officer candidates will experience many aspects of soldiering, including road marches, night patrols, rifle marksmanship, and several nights in the cold, foggy Fort Lewis, field without benefit of a sleeping bag.*

BELOW *The payoff for all that study and suffering is a pair of gold bars ("butter bars" in the vernacular) denoting a second lieutenant in the U.S.Army, in this case presented by Col. Holbrook to 2nd Lt. Holbrook. There's an old tradition that is now to be followed – the officer, when he receives his first salute from an enlisted soldier, must present to that soldier a silver dollar.*

They "cammie up" and make ruck marches. They go to the field and eat MREs for five straight days, learning about conducting night patrols and raids, using land navigation with map and compass, even though many of them will never employ these skills again. They will try to sleep in a field-expedient sleeping bag assembled from a poncho and poncho liner, a difficult thing to do in Fort Lewis' chilly summer fog and damp.

West Point and the Long Gray Line

The United States Military Academy at West Point, New York, is still the most demanding program for preparing men and women for service as Army officers. In some ways the USMA is just another four-year school with a rigorous academic program and a reputation for building good engineers. More than that, however, West Point breeds a special kind of Army officer, the legendary "ring-knocker," a young man or woman with exceptionally high motivation, dedication, and discipline, a survivor of a long ordeal, and someone who doesn't let anybody else forget it.

The class ring worn by USMA grads is heavy, in more ways than one. In staff conferences, graduates have sometimes, perhaps unconsciously, made their points in debate a bit stronger by tapping that big ring on the table by way of emphasis. Intentional or not, this legendary habit has been interpreted as a non-verbal way of saying: "Although we may all be [for example] captains, my opinion carries more weight than yours because I went to West Point." West Point graduates have a reputation for supreme self confidence, great "school-house-solution" ability, a somewhat condescending attitude toward subordinate officers, and a remote attitude toward enlisted soldiers.

This attitude of superiority is actually earned. Standards for everything at the Academy are higher than in the rest of the Army and to complete the program requires a cadet to hold him or herself to a higher mark. If West Pointers consider themselves better prepared to be an officer, a lot of officers from other programs agree with them, at least for some skills and some kinds of leadership.

It is also the most difficult program for an aspiring officer candidate to join. Only about 1,000 young men are accepted each year, along with about 200 young women. For those coming directly from high school, the process is a brutal shock. "Plebes," or first year cadets, are thrown into a world of spartan discipline that is extreme by any military measure; not even student Green Berets must ask permission to eat, or sit in extreme postures at meals.

This month-long period is called Beast Barracks and takes all the pressure and stress of the enlisted recruit's Basic Training and doubles it. The stress here is somewhat like the first part of the training for Green Berets or SEALs—it is turned way up in an attempt to see who the weaklings are so that they might be quickly discarded. Plebes mostly learn how to stand up straight and how to follow commands instantly. Each learns to "make chins" and to salute with a crispness unknown anywhere else in the Army. Uniforms are hung in closets with great care and to exacting tolerances, but seldom with quite enough precision to satisfy the Tactical Officer, or TAC. It takes very little time at all before some of the new plebes have had enough and decide to quit in favor of some quiet liberal arts college, and that's just fine

with the TACs. Beast Barracks ends with a 15-mile ruck march that begins at 0300. The cadets who make it back to the hallowed halls of the Academy have won their first victory.

During the next four years, while other college students are getting blitzed on weekends and aren't all that sober during the week, West Point cadets begin their days at 0530, end them at midnight, and are performing to a sober and very high standard every minute in between. Cadets pursue one of 24 possible majors, all technical, and are required to be competitive athletes as well. During summers they are required to participate in military training and other

LEFT: *Soldiers do very few things alone, including suffer. This is hot, filthy, exhausting recruit training in the humid Georgia summer, but instead of breaking these soldiers down, it builds them up, individually and as members of a kind of extended family. Adversity builds character and the Army applies physical and intellectual challenges to its neophytes in the officer and enlisted classes as part of a controlled process to prepare each individual for the rigors of warfare.*

OPPOSITE, ABOVE: *By the time an officer makes full colonel, or pay grade O-6, he or she can look back on a long and successful career; very, very few newly commissioned lieutenants will wear eagles. The ones that do, as with Col. Allen, the 4th Infantry Division's artillery commander here, also look ahead, shaping the force of the future.*

OPPOSITE, BELOW: *Lt. Col. Tim Wray with two of his company commanders during field training. Junior officers are mentored by their commanders, and the most talented are groomed and prepared for greater responsibilities as majors and lieutenant colonels. No matter how high the rank they achieve, most cherish their early troop commands as lieutenants and captains.*

activities; some will go to Airborne or Air Assault schools while others supervise incoming plebes.

West Point has, over its two centuries, developed its own language, culture, and tradition, a place where everyone knows who a "Firstie" is, and when your "Cow Summer" begins and ends. The USMA hasn't produced all the Army's top officers, but some of the most distinguished—Generals Grant, Eisenhower, Patton, Lee, MacArthur, and Schwarzkopf, among many others—and more as a percentage of its graduates than ROTC or OCS. That heritage is one kind of "long gray line," and the ghosts of those history-making, war-winning, legendary ring-knockers sit heavily on the shoulders of West Point graduates throughout their entire careers, for better or worse.

Seeing Stars—Command, Staff, and Jedi Knights

For officers, the profession of arms involves a predictable sequence of schools, commands, promotions, and responsibility—if they are both gifted and lucky. A newly

ABOVE LEFT: *Sergeants have their own leadership roles and responsibilities, and command sergeants major like Russ Mann, a "Green Beret" with extensive combat experience in Viet Nam, are a buffer between senior officers and junior enlisted soldiers.*

ABOVE: *Staff Sgt. Christopher Dumont directs his soldiers as they use cover and concealment to approach a bunker complex. The mission is to clear the position, something they will do with grenades, supporting fires, and maneuver.*

RIGHT: *This soldier is a sergeant E-5 and a PRD-11 radio direction finder used by electronic warfare units.*

minted "butter-bar" goes to the Officer Basic Course and is trained in the fundamentals of his or her branch specialty. Then it is off, normally, to a line unit and the first practical test of all that preparation. For infantry officers, for example, this will mean command of a platoon along with collateral duties. The new lieutenant learns how it works in the real

world, partly from the more senior officers in the company, partly from the sergeants. A new officer quickly learns that there is "officers' work" and "sergeants' work," and old NCOs are not shy about showing new lieutenants where they think that line is drawn.

Learning to lead is a little different from learning to administer an organization, and gaining the respect of the soldiers takes time and demonstrated ability. The old Army tradition is that an officer is supposed to be capable of doing anything he or she asks of the troops, whether that involves running five miles with a 40-pound ruck, making up a range card for a machine gun, or any other chore. An officer should be competent to do anything those in his or her unit are required to do, and more.

As with the enlisted ranks, there are layers of responsibility, authority, rank, and respect for officers. During the required four or five years of service following commissioning, an officer will be promoted to first lieutenant (Pay Grade O-2) and possibly to Captain O-3. These are the "company" grades. Somewhere within this first enlistment will be, normally, an opportunity to command soldiers, and an opportunity for more schooling. During this period each officer's commanders will be watching him or her intently. Each will regularly write an Officer Evaluation Report (OER) that candidly describes the vices and virtues of the officer, and these reports can be vicious. One such adverse report can easily mean the end of a career or the loss of a promotion, and the farther up the food chain an officer progresses, the more critical these reports are likely to be.

Command and General Staff College

But when an officer does well, with glittering OERs, promotions come along rapidly and early. A major's gold oak leaves are the reward and the entry into the "field grade" ranks of the officer class. If selected for lieutenant colonel (O-5) after around 15 years of service, officers are beginning to become part of the upper reaches of middle management. If they've done well so far, it is off to grad school—the Command and General Staff College at Fort Leavenworth, Kansas. Here the Army prepares its leaders for commanding combat brigades and for leading the charge into the future.

SAMS and Jedi Knights

Since its inception in the early 1980s, fast-track officers get tapped to attend the School of Advanced Military Studies, called SAMS. These leaders have shown talent for command all through their careers and now it begins to pay off. They are typically very young lieutenant colonels, alert, confident, and energetic. Only 72 officers from all branches of the American armed forces are selected for this year-long course. SAMS is a place where the Army's best and brightest are groomed for the highest positions of leadership, and these

are the officers who will shape the force of the future. They are known throughout the Army as Jedi Knights.

SAMS was a response to what was, 20 years ago, perceived to be a lack of training for senior officers in strategic and operational planning—the theory, history, and doctrine of modern war. The program involves six seminars, detailed study of previous battles and campaigns and a lot of reading of the classics of military literature. Distinguished scholars, authors, and other guest speakers address SAMS students.

Terrain walks are another feature of SAMS—a guided tour of historic battlegrounds conducted by extremely knowledgeable historian soldiers. Among these have recently been Gettysburg and the Wilderness campaigns. In small groups, the SAMS officers "walk the ground" where critical combat decisions have been made, for better or worse. Sometimes, too, they can be pulled into active military operations. SAMS attendees helped develop the "end-run" strategy used so successfully against Iraq's forces during the Gulf War.

Part of this program is a sabbatical during which individual officers study a topic of their choice, then write a monograph on the subject. Each is quizzed by a board of very senior officers. Finally, they receive a Master of Military Arts and Science degree. Army officers successfully completing SAMS are typically assigned to the planning cell of a division or other major command. They are also likely to be promoted to Colonel (O-6) much earlier than other lieutenant colonels. Attendance doesn't guarantee the single star of a brigadier general (O-7), but it helps.

BNOC

Back in the old Army, soldiers were promoted up from the ranks into the mid-level NCO corps by simply re-enlisting once. Promotions were essentially automatic, based on time in grade and vacancies within the unit, but not any more. Today's soldier has to study harder than a pre-med student, pass written and oral tests, and then survive a rigorous training program called the Basic Noncommissioned Officer Course, popularly known as BNOC.

These BNOC academies are found on most major Army installations around the world. The duration of the course is typically about one month during which students learn skills common to all NCOs around the Army as well as specific duties for their MOS. Each learns the fine points of close-

RIGHT: *Up, up and away! Before making their first parachute jump, Airborne students get a thrill ride that comes close to the real thing from the 250-foot tower. With the canopy attached to a large ring, the student is hoisted aloft, then released to float down again, hopefully demonstrating perfect "prepare to land" and PLF techniques.*

This is individual training, based on decades of
experience, the lessons of combat as well as millions
of training jumps, all designed to make individual
soldiers qualified to join teams of other qualified
soldiers. Then they will train to work as units – in
this case, as members of units conducting Airborne
operations – the 82nd Airborne Division and
XVIII Airborne Corps, 75th Ranger Regiment,
and the Special Forces groups.

order drill and ceremony, "voice of command," and rotates through leadership positions within the class – student squad leader, platoon sergeant, and first sergeant.

The training includes classroom instruction on administration, regulations, and the paperwork required to manage a military unit. Students spend a lot of time in ranks, being inspected. They go to the field, to learn small unit leadership skills and then demonstrate them.

Airborne School

Many thousands of soldiers attend Fort Benning's Basic Airborne Course and become qualified military parachutists, although for most it is just a ticket punch—they will never serve in a unit that could actually jump into a combat zone. And despite occasional claims to the contrary, this three-week program has been severely modified in recent years in ways that would make the old-time paratroopers cringe in dismay. One of the "Black Hats," as the instructors are called, told me recently that it has become "… three weeks of low-impact aerobics." That's not quite true, but almost anybody can get through the runs and PT, including some very small (under 4-foot 6-inches) and very weak people. Everybody has to run two miles at about an eight-minute-mile pace, just a bit slower than the days of yore, but virtually no Airborne student today does pull-ups to the old standard, and the weakest are permitted to have someone actually give them a boost! Gone are the beloved Gig Pit where students used to get extra attention from kindly Sergeant Airborne and learned how to do push-ups and sit-ups to perfection. But you still have to jump out of an airplane, and not everybody is willing to try.

Week One is Ground Week. Students begin the day with a run at 0500, then about 45 minutes of PT, return to their barracks for chow, then are back in ranks by 0715 or so. The ever-friendly Black Hats often find fault with some of the students' alignment in ranks or politely point out some other deficiency, and thoughtfully help the aspirants correct these problems, normally with push-ups on the gravel. The deficient student is prevented from feeling lonely or picked upon during this by the tradition of having everybody do push-ups for anybody's errors. This tradition goes back to the beginning of the school in World War II.

Another tradition is "The Keeper of the Wings." Early in Week One, the "first shirt" for each training company will call the youngest student out of formation and up onto the platform. This is almost always a baby-faced 17-year-old private right out of Basic. This very young soldier is called to attention facing the class, some of whom are old enough to be his parents. The First Sergeant produces the "jump wings" badge that will be awarded to graduates of the course after their fifth jump and holds it up for all to see. Then this set of jump wings is pinned inside the student's pocket. The

ABOVE: *Pvt. Margareta Colocho is a cook and, at 4ft 6in tall, not the image of the traditional paratrooper. Yet the Basic Airborne Course is open to her and nearly all soldiers, young and old, male and female, and is not restricted to any MOS. Old soldiers attend, too, some in their forties, and the parachutist badge is a measure of accomplishment for all of them.*

ABOVE RIGHT: *"November One Four Six" is a sergeant who has been in the Army a while and is now becoming "jump quali-fied." One of the famous Black Hats, as the instructors are called, performs the JMPI ritual that insures his equipment is properly fitted, snaps buckled correctly, static line (the yellow strap) properly routed, with its pins in their cones. The process still happens at the same place it began sixty years ago, at Lawson Army Air Field on Fort Benning, Georgia.*

RIGHT AND FAR RIGHT: *The first two jumps are done in daylight, without combat equipment – "Hollywood" jumps, the soldier call them. Nobody gets through the course without making five jumps, one of which is supposed to be at night and two with rucksack and weapons container. There are occasional injuries, but not many, and occasional "refusals" of a student to go out the door, but both are rare.*

Keeper of the Wings is required to keep this badge highly polished and ready for inspection at any moment, day or night, by any of the Sergeants Airborne. If, for any reason, the Keeper of the Wings is dropped from the class, the wings are passed to the next-junior student.

During this first week, students become acquainted with the T-10 parachute, especially with its harness, neither of which have changed very much in the last 50 years. They learn how to don and adjust the main parachute, how to put on the reserve, and how to fit the harness. They learn everything there is to know about what to do inside the aircraft, how to exit, proper body position, reserve deployment, and push-ups. They will do endless PLFs—the "parachute landing fall" maneuver that reduces the chance of injury when you come down to earth—and they will make mistakes, and do more push-ups.

By the end of the week, most are sore all over and grateful for a weekend to recover. Week Two is Tower Week where the training is taken to a new and higher level. Each day begins with the run and PT, but now the students start working with the Swing Landing Trainer and the 34-foot tower. All of them go out of the tower dozens of times, learning how to exit an aircraft through the side door. Later in the week they may get to try the thrilling 250-foot tower and a ride under a real canopy. The ever-kindly sergeants never forget to help all the students perfect their push-up techniques and offer helpful advice to any students that need it.

Week Three is Jump Week. Now it all comes together for real, with real parachutes and real aircraft. On Monday of Week Three, the students are marched down to Lawson Field early in the morning. They get chow from the back of a truck, then draw their parachutes while one or two Air Force C-130s await them. The students nervously don the parachutes and are carefully inspected, one at a time, by the cadre, a ritual called the "jumpmaster personnel inspection." When everybody has been JMPIed, and if the weather is good, and the aircraft working properly, there comes the command, "On your feet!"

They are marched out to the aircraft in "stick" order, with the last jumper out being the first to board. The engines are already running and the memorable perfume of hot JP-5 exhaust fills the air along with vast quantities of adrenaline. Soon after first light (the gods and Air Force permitting) the Hercules taxis out from the same field, from the same runway, where it all began so long, and so many thousands of jump students, ago.

Out on Fryer Drop Zone, across the Chattahoochie River, the Drop Zone Safety Officer and a squad of

RIGHT: *The Ranger tab is the mark of a man who has been through an ordeal worthy of the Spartans – weeks of extreme pressure, with long periods with little food or sleep.*

FAR RIGHT: *One way to wake up a class of exhausted Mountain Phase students is to throw something unexpected at them, and what could be more unexpected that a couple of naked guys running through the training area.*

Black Hats are ready. So is an ambulance. The pilot makes a first pass, drops a wind-drift indicator and gets a radio call from the DZSO clearing the first jump pass. The pilot will fly a large "race-track" pattern, come back for the first jump run, offset from the centerline of the DZ just enough to put the jumpers in the middle of Fryer.

The crew gives the jumpmaster a five minute warning. He faces the stick and commands, over the roar of the aircraft, "OUTBOARD PERSONNEL, STAND UP!" The door control is actuated and it slides up, out of the way. Inside the plane the excitement level is near the top of everybody's scale. The jumpmaster sticks his head out the door, monitoring progress, then commands, "HOOK UP!" while giving the visual signal to attach static lines. The jumpers (the ones that are tall enough, anyway) attach their yellow static lines to the cable overhead, insert a wire safety pin, and collect the slack in the line into a bight held in the inboard hand.

In the aircraft, the jumpmaster opens his side door and sticks his head out in the icy blast to monitor progress. He pops back in and gives the verbal and hand signal, "CHECK EQUIPMENT!" All the jumpers repeat the command, as they have all the others, and inspect the harness, helmet, and ruck of the jumper in front of them, being inspected in return. When the last jumper in the stick is ready, he or she yells "OKAY" and swats the next jumper in line until the command comes back to the jumpmaster, who then commands, "STAND IN THE DOOR!" The first student assumes the door position that they've been practicing for the last two weeks—with the novel addition now of 1,250 feet of open air below, the cool blast of the slipstream outside, and with adrenal glands working at capacity. The jumpmaster waits till the aircraft passes the leading edge of the DZ, turns to the first jumper, points to the door, and commands, "GO!" From there to the ground, everything is pretty much automatic, with a little help from the Black Hats who coach the students using bullhorns. "Check canopy, check canopy, check canopy!" they command.

ABOVE RIGHT: *The Ranger program tests students in multiple ways at the same time – physical stress is part of it, with huge rucksack loads, fast marches, and broken terrain. On top of that, though, and most important, students have to work together effectively, make good decisions, execute their mission, on limited food, limited sleep, and unlimited challeges from the Ranger Instructors.*

RIGHT: *Here's an easy part of the problem – just climb the ladder, wait for the command, then run along the plank, up and over the steps, then to the cable. Now, on command, grasp the trapeze, hold on until you hit the water. Some students hit the water before getting to the cable, and that's a No Go.*

Each student will make five jumps during the week, three "Hollywood" jumps without combat equipment, one or two so-called combat jumps (but with light rucks and weapons containers very much unlike those used on actual combat jumps), and one night jump. The night jump is often conducted during twilight instead of full darkness.

There are, very rarely, students who balk and refuse to jump but most pour out the door exactly as they've been doing since Ground Week. More often, some jumpers are injured, nearly always from poor PLFs, and are attended to by the medics. Twisted ankles are pretty common, broken bones less so but a hazard.

At the end of the week, after the fifth jump, they are formed up and jump wings pinned on by the now-friendly Black Hats. Some, particularly second or third generation Airborne students, have the wings pinned on by their fathers—or, often now—their mothers.

Rangers Lead the Way

How curious it is that, in a time when modern technology—"smart" bombs, digital communications, night vision systems, automatic targeting systems, Chobham armor, fire-and-forget missiles—is so important that the Army would revere and maintain and promote a set of military skills and values that are nearly unchanged from those of hundreds and even thousands of years ago. The Ranger program is like that, a place that sorts out men who have a kind of personal integrity that isn't visible anywhere else in American society. What's more, the products of this program are one very essential part of the arsenal of weapons the president and the "national command authority" depend upon whenever push comes to shove.

There are basically two kinds of Rangers in the Army, and both go through the same program, operated by Fort Benning and the Infantry School's Ranger Training Brigade (RTB). Both have gone through the same ordeal, but some will take the experience and the training back to other combat-arms units in artillery, armor, infantry, engineer, or other branches, while a select few will join the fabled 75th Ranger Regiment. Each will wear a simple black and gold tab on the left shoulder reading simply "RANGER." But every soldier in the Army appreciates that the Ranger tab identifies a man who has been through a form of hell and come out the other side stronger and smarter, a living example of Army values. Rangers lead the way for the whole Army, literally and figuratively.

The Benning Phase, Part One and Two

The actual sequence of individual events varies from year to year, commander to commander, but here's how it works. There are three phases, each brutal in a special way. The first one is conducted out in the back woods of Fort Benning in the Harmony Church area away from the distractions of main post. It begins very early on a Monday morning with a PT test—49 perfect push-ups, 53 perfect sit-ups, and a two-mile run at a brisk 7-minutes, 36-seconds per mile pace. The Ranger instructors are merciless about these exercises, accepting nothing less than perfection, and pushing all the students hard during the run. Pull-ups follow, but unlike on the Basic Airborne Course, you can't get help from a buddy—these are the old-fashioned kind, from a fully extended arm, all the way up, without swinging or pumping.

For those who last past the PT test, there is the Combat Water Survival Test, hand-to-hand combat training, with and without pugil sticks, bayonet training, land nav classes and

This Ranger "kindergarten" phase includes one parachute jump, some patrolling, a bit of demolition training, and the ever-thrilling Water Confidence Test at Victory Pond. This latter event isn't all that hard physically—you just climb up about 30 feet to a beam that is only a few inches wide. When the Ranger instructor tells you, walk the beam about 20 feet, go up and down a couple of stairs, just to keep you on your toes, and then walk another 20 feet or so. It would be easy except you do all this up in space and a misstep means a long fall. At the end of the beam is a cable on which rides a trapeze bar; on command, grasp the bar and ride the trapeze down to the water. This event is just one of the many ordeals Ranger students endure, but they don't do it alone, and the

tests, plus lots of 3-mile ruck runs, occasional 5-mile ruck runs, and a 16-mile ruck march. The program is never exactly the same from one class to another, but no matter what is happening, it will be a challenge. Students suffer from sleep-deprivation, getting sometimes just an hour or two per day. They are intentionally malnourished, during much of the course only getting three MREs (about 4,000 calories) for two days of extremely strenuous activity. They will lose a lot of weight, often between 20 and 40 pounds in about nine weeks. They'll hallucinate and bleed and never know what's coming next. Broken bones are common. But much of that is yet to come during the first part of the Benning phase.

instructors show them how easy it is—they run along the beam, stop to do push-ups, and generally show off.

Still within the Benning phase, survivors move on to an intense period of training on small unit patrolling and raids—living in the field, planning and executing operations, writing and giving op orders, learning to execute ambushes, clearing buildings, sitting still in the dark, and trying to sneak bits of food when the Ranger Instructors don't seem to be watching.

The instructors watch carefully, and will evaluate each student, eliminating many of them for one deficiency or another. But the students evaluate each other, too, and peer

A Soldier's Legacy

Unlike a carpenter or tradesman who creates tangible things, a soldier creates his or her own legacy. When you lead or train subordinates, you change them in positive and negative ways. At the end of the day, one way or the other, what you have accomplished as a soldier leader is the imprinting of your own set of attitudes, values, and skills onto your soldiers, your peers and superiors alike. Soldiers are keenly aware that they are the products of those who came before - the soldiers who led and trained us, as well as those who led and trained them, going all the way back to the beginning of our history.

An Army of "Us"

The current Army recruiting theme is "An Army of One." Few people that I know in the Army like that theme - there is no such thing as "An Army of One." Appealing to the individuality of today's young people might be necessary to get their attention, but once they get here, they find that it is "An Army of Us." Naturally, before joining the Army they think mostly about themselves. But once they become soldiers, they must try and measure up to those around them, those who came before, and finally the Army Legacy.

Planners and Executors - Officers and Enlisted

Generally speaking, the officer corps conceives the plan and the enlisted soldier executes the plan. As an enlisted soldier, I routinely executed plans that my experience and intellect told me were flawed, and not likely to be successful – I was set up for failure on too many occasions even before we crossed the "LD." [Line of Departure, the place where the active phase of a combat mission begins.] These kinds of experiences were what encouraged me to attend the Officer Candidate School (OCS) and obtain a commission. I was a Staff Sergeant (E-6) and painfully realized that Sergeants were more than capable of planning and then executing missions without additional adult supervision. An example: within Special Operations Communities around the world, you will find small expertly trained teams composed entirely of Non Commissioned Officers. Our own Special Forces (SF) A-Teams are composed almost entirely of Senior NCOs. I believe that the single officer on a forward-deployed SF team is there as a buffer and figurehead. He is the diplomatic representative of the United States Government and isn't any better qualified to plan and then execute operations than the sergeants on the team. Realistically he is probably not as good at his business as the men he leads.

OCS

I was too old and un-educated for any other commissioning program. OCS is the best program in the Army. Unfortunately, it is also a well-kept secret. It differs from both the Reserve Officer Training Corps and the West Point commissioning programs in that nothing about it is very difficult by itself, but the stress level of everything together is intense. And, for those of us who entered as accomplished Non Commissioned Officers (NCOs) having to humiliate your self before the cadre can be an added stress. That stress often does not seem to have a purpose. We were running around, one time, about two in the morning, doing something useless, and I asked my cadre NCO, "Sergeant, what are we doing this for?" He said, "Candidate, if it was easy, everybody would be an officer."

Rangers

I've been a Ranger for over eight years. We are held to a special standard that is a bit more demanding than that of the regular Army – a higher commitment to others that is learned during Ranger training. As a Ranger, you are pledged to never fail the other Rangers on your team, or your mission, unto death. In the forefront of every Ranger's mind is the individual responsibility to others in the group, a sense of duty that goes back to 1756, to Roger's Rangers and long before American independence from Britain. Just as with the Green Berets and SEALs, you aren't fully a member of the Ranger Community just because you graduated from the training program – you must daily prove yourself to the members of your Ranger Unit. Only then are you really a Ranger.

FAR LEFT: *Day One for a new class of Ranger students; it isn't even light yet and they've run five hard, fast miles and are already deep into a class on hand to hand combat. The class has already lost several members and will lose many more in the next few days.*

ABOVE LEFT: *Rangers have been relying on ropes in combat since World War II and used them to complete their D-Day missions on 6 June 1944. Today, Rangers are adept at fast-roping from helicopters, an insertion technique that is one of the many combat skills required of individual Rangers.*

The Ranger Mission Today

Today's Rangers missions are like those of a SWAT team on steroids – a bit different from the kinds of infantry type raids and assaults in our past. Until about 1992, the emphasis was on advanced light infantry tactics. Conducting lightning fast raids and ambushing the enemy deep in the woods, gave way to attacking buildings and performing blocking operations for the Special Operations Detachment-DELTA in and around built up areas.
Captain Charles Greene, US Army Ranger

reviews are brutal for anyone who is perceived as not pulling his weight, or cheating in any way. Officers train alongside the enlisted soldiers, unlike in other Army schools, and are cut no slack by either the cadre or the soldiers when it is time for evaluations, and you can pass all the tests but if your peers don't think you've been meeting spec, you're going home. At the end of about three weeks, the class will be much smaller than at the beginning, and survivors are transported to the rocky hills of North Georgia.

Mountain Phase

The food is good and plentiful up at the Mountain Phase at Camp Frank D. Merrill, near Dahlonega, Georgia, and the students will be loafing around, getting up to five hours sleep per night. At Dahlonega, every student leads, and every student follows, regardless of rank. They make ruck marches with heavier rucks, and up hill. There are classes on military aspects of mountaineering, with students learning rope work, knots, and all variations on rappelling. They make and use rope bridges to cross streams and rocky gorges. They will all have been rappelling for years, but now they'll get a chance to try advanced techniques like the face-down Australian method, and they'll bring a Stokes litter and patient down a rock wall. They will learn, practice, and be tested on their climbing technique. They will work on patrolling again, this time in mountainous terrain. There is a four day squad FTX (field training exercise) and a five-day platoon FTX, both complete with an opposing force (OPFOR) who will try to make life even more miserable for the students.

All that mountaineering training gets a workout as the students conduct helicopter insertions, cross-country movements, raids and ambushes against vehicles and structures. Then they carry their rucks on a long march over the Tennessee Valley Divide. That would be difficult enough, but the Ranger Instructors (RIs) continually challenge the students by throwing missions at them, relieving one from command and pulling somebody else out of the ranks, and sending them off to do difficult missions when they are all ready to drop. At the end of another two weeks, they will again be evaluated by their peers and by their instructors, and the class will have shrunk a bit more.

Ranger School

"In Ranger School, just knowing I had an MRE in my ruck was often more than enough, almost better than eating it. When I would finally break it out to enjoy just a portion [remember, when you are only getting three MREs for every two days in the field, you should not eat the whole thing in just a single sitting] I would liken it to setting up a small shrine. A typical scenario follows:

"After a mission, we would move off the objective and set a patrol base for the night. Sounds simple, but this usually occurred around 0300–0400ish with first call at 0500–0600ish. Obviously, sleep was a premium; however, my first priority was to enjoy an 'evening meal' prior to sleeping. The SOP (Standard Operating Procedure) was to set my rucksack down so that the frame faced me. Then I would pull out the MRE and place my poncho liner over the ruck and myself, with a red lens Mini-Maglight clipped to the visor of my PC (patrol cap) creating the shrine. Then, using just the right mix of 'ingredients,' the preparation and enjoyment of the MRE could occur. Notice I say enjoyment because to me, there was no worse waste of this precious food than to wolf it down while on the move, not seasoned with Tabasco Sauce and salt, and not diluted with as much water as humanly possible to try and make it seem like more food than you actually had. Finally once I had carefully and painstakingly eaten and savored every bite, I would take my Leatherman knife, carefully cut the envelope open, lick the blade, and proceed to lick the envelope so clean that even the ants could not find a morsel of food.

"Many different recipes floated about the circle of the Ranger students. Standard ones included the main meal (beef stew, corned beef hash, ham slice, etc.) mixed with water, Tabasco Sauce, and salt. Perhaps, crackers and cheese could be added depending on if they were needed for other recipes. An example of this would be for the infamous 'Ranger Pudding.' There are many variations, from the simplest (crushed crackers mixed with cocoa beverage powder and a very slight amount of water) up to the most elaborate one that required saving items from several MREs to create (the aforementioned crackers, cocoa, and water along with coffee, creamer, sugar, peanut butter, and M&Ms). Other delicacies included cheesecake (crushed crackers, beverage-based powder other than lemon-lime (not a good cheesecake flavor), cheese, and water) and the chocolate éclair (the RIs made a mistake and issued us a few of the shelf-stable bread supplements and no word of lie, the bread with a covering of cocoa beverage powder mixed with a little bit of water and coffee, creamer, and sugar tastes just like a bakery éclair).

"Ways to eat your MRE had to be creative, because the RIs 'highly frowned' upon eating during other-than-authorized periods. This coupled with the distinct and pungent odor of certain MRE items could obviously

LEFT: *Going up and over the cargo net station is just one simple part of the obstacle course for Special Forces students at Camp MacKall, North Carolina, and one of the easiest, too.*

spell disaster. The cheese falls into this category, as one Ranger student found out the hard way in Florida phase. While waiting to carry out a river crossing, the patrol was supposed to be conducting security. However, a student opened a cheese packetto snack on while waiting. Moments later, even in the pitch-black and unable to see anything, the entire patrol along with multiple RIs could not help but smell that a cheese packet had been opened. All I remember in the dark was the RI shouting 'Whoever the f*** just opened his MRE while we are supposed to be on security, come f***ing see me. You are getting a f***ing spot report.' Everyone did it—ate while on security—you just did not want to be the one to get caught.

"My TTP [literally translates to Tactics, Techniques, and Procedures, but used as slang for a way to do something in the Army] for snacking while on security was more covert. When pulling security from the hasty fighting positions in the Desert phase, we were issued training Claymores [mines] to place out from the patrol base. Once the Claymores had been placed, you were left with an empty Claymore bag along with the clacker and test set at your position. I quickly figured out that cutting the seam between the two pockets made it easier to get the mine in and out. However, this also provided a perfect pouch to put a prepared main meal in to snack on (assuming it was cut lengthwise as opposed to being opened on the narrow side where the Army places the starter cuts and most novices open it). Then, when an RI would come up on your position, you would simply flip the pouch cover closed and voilà, you were diligently

pulling security with no distracting food to lessen your alertness. I never got a negative spot report for food, although I did get my share for other debacles."

Florida Phase

Now begins another part of the ordeal, three more weeks of hell, but this time in steamy, slimy Florida. Students who are already Airborne qualified will parachute in, the rest will arrive by bus. By this time virtually all the students are heavily stressed, have lost a lot of weight, and are suffering the effects of prolonged sleep deprivation. This pressure tests the resolve of each; it is very easy to turn it all off by simply failing to keep up on one of the runs, something that appears a bit more honorable than simply quitting. As this pressure continues to take its toll, some student Rangers will occasionally cheat by finding shortcuts or ways to lighten a rucksack. These are honor violations and result in immediate dismissal.

Each student is tested in many ways, and all will fail somehow, sometime. If you've been awake for 70 of the past 72 hours, pulling security in the middle of an inky black night is an invitation to fall asleep, and almost unavoidable. That same lack of sleep, plus malnutrition and tactical stress, inhibits good decision-making skills for both followers and leaders. So, naturally, the RIs continually challenge the exhausted students by swapping out leadership roles, by changing the mission, by throwing simulated artillery bombardments, to see who bends and who breaks.

During Phase One, the students brushed up on individual skills. During Phase Two, squad operations were the primary focus. The Florida Phase emphasizes platoon

patrol operations, first in training, then in a ten-day FTX. Now they execute raids, long-range infil and exfil ops over land and by small boat. A talented OPFOR prowls the jungle looking for them, and ambushes and assaults occur frequently. There is little time for food or rest, and many opportunities for making mistakes. By now, though, the remaining students are the tough ones and likely to make it through to the end. At the end of another three weeks, up to 40 pounds lighter, the students will make one more parachute jump, this time back into Fort Benning where they will be awarded their Ranger tabs.

One Ranger graduate says of the program:
"I would say that it is the best small unit training the Army has, an excellent test of mental toughness, and somewhat physically demanding, although most who go are in top physical condition. Attitude and motivation, along with decision making under stressful conditions, are the real tests. Peer evaluations also result in quite a few not making it through. You cannot be a guy who likes being in the spotlight if you want to make it through—only soldiers who are always contributing to the mission, never complaining, will succeed. I remember the blueberry pancakes at the mess hall during the mountain phase, the weight of the M60 machine gun I carried, and going eyeball-to-eyeball with a poisonous water moccasin snake during one patrol in Florida."

Another reports:
"My personal recollections of Ranger School are numerous and, now that it is a long time ago, funny. For example, during a map check, I peed on my Ranger Instructor, my Assistant Patrol Leader and my Radio operator—that was in Darby Phase. [The Darby Phase of Ranger School is held near Fort Benning, Georgia, at Camp William O. Darby. It is the second major part of the course.] *I was so hungry that I dumpster-dove for a half eaten (at least one week old) cheeseburger in the Florida Phase. I was caught sleeping in a wall locker by a grumpy Ranger Instructor in 'city week' (Darby). I stole a Snickers candy bar in the Mountain Phase, and my whole squad helped me eat it out of solidarity. (I later sent the 'little store' in Dahlonega a $5.00 check for my guilt). I sleep-walked in the MTN Phase, and I screwed up so many other times that I can't remember them all. And, I was the enlisted honor graduate of my course! What I personally got out of Ranger School was the discovered ability to push well past my own established limits, both physical and mental. Additionally, for a Private First Class in the 3rd Ranger Battalion, it was a great vacation away from a place where everybody who out-ranked you seemed to hate you and treated you accordingly!"*

Very Special Forces

From the very beginning, the Army's Special Forces—the guys almost everybody calls the "Green Berets"—have been special people with a special set of missions quite different from the rest of the Army. The men (they are all men) who

are selected for SF training and who make it through to wear the green beret have the mental toughness of Rangers, but have other skill sets and talents not needed in conventional soldiering.

Green Berets are the Army's behind-the-lines evangelists, missionaries with a military mission. They are trained to operate in tiny groups, far from friends, in the middle of exotic and sometimes hostile cultures. In groups of only a dozen, they can recruit, train, administer, command, and lead a whole battalion of unconventional soldiers. During World War II, they worked with the French resistance and with guerrillas in Burma, during Vietnam they had a long love affair with the stone-age hill tribes, and more recently they've grown beards and ridden horses with Afghan irregulars. While apprentice Rangers learn all the approved ways to kill people and destroy things, SF soldiers learn how to be diplomats with rifles and how to charm their way to victory.

Officers and enlisted soldiers become qualified for the Special Forces tab and the green beret by going through a four-part program operated by the Special Warfare Center and School at Fort Bragg, North Carolina. Until recently, an applicant for SF training had to have a lot of time in the Army, in grade E-4 to E-7, be pretty mature (believe it or not), and on at least a second enlistment. Currently, though, the Army is allowing male recruits to specify SF as an enlistment option, and the first of these are now going through the Qualification (or "Q") Course. These soldiers are much younger than the men who traditionally go

through the program, and have almost no military foundation, but early reports from the NCOs running the program indicate that these students are actually doing pretty well—much to the surprise of cadre and veterans both.

Since the process of selecting and training the one soldier in a thousand who can make it all the way through the Q Course and earn a beret is very expensive, the Army added a preliminary phase of the course designed to weed out the men who, for whatever reason, aren't going to get through. This is called the SFAS, or Special Forces Assessment and Selection Course, and it is three intense weeks of physical and mental challenges. A surprising number of applicants are eliminated almost immediately, either on the ruck runs (they are called marches but if you walk you won't meet the time requirement so running is essential) or on the swim test. Soldiers who are otherwise in superb physical condition often sink to the bottom of the pool, utterly unable to stay afloat or complete the 50-meter swim in boots and BDUs. The ruck runs are fiendish—the students don't know how far they have to go, or how fast; they keep moving from one checkpoint to another until somebody tells them it is over and they've passed or failed. The physical stress is magnified by the uncertainty of the ordeal. Attrition in SFAS is high, but that's fine with the cadre—better now than later.

Only after passing SFAS and being recommended by a board does the real training begin, a process that will last up to 18 months for medics and at least six months for other enlisted students. The first phase of training is held at Camp Mackall,

FAR LEFT, INSET: *Although known by the public as "Green Berets," the proper and preferred name for this organization is Special Forces. The SF tab is a distinction and the mark of a very special soldier.*

FAR LEFT: *Rappelling is an important military skill in all of the special operational forces, useful in air operations, urban combat, and in mountainous terrain. The tower at Camp MacKall, with its vertical wall on the right and helicopter skid on the left, gets plenty of use.*

LEFT: *Special Forces engineers learn how to build things and to take them apart. Of the two, the second is much more fun. That's because SF engineers are adept at the use of explosives in many forms, including military dynamite and TNT, shown here.*

an austere facility near Fort Bragg and lasts about 40 days. Most of this part of the course is similar to Ranger training—lots of patrol skills, lots of land nav training and tests, constant stress, little sleep, and lots of surprises.

Then, for those who last, comes MOS training. There are five basic specialties, beginning with the officers preparing to lead an A detachment. These are the 18-Alphas who attend a 24-week course held at Fort Bragg and Fort A.P. Hill, Virginia.

Weapons specialists are the 18-Bravos. They also spend 24 weeks in a qualification program. Theirs includes training on dozens of types of small arms and crew-served weapons. Almost any RPG, anti-tank missile, rifle, pistol, machine gun, carbine, or grenade found in any nation's arsenal will be studied by the Bravos. They are adept at maintaining all these weapons and at firing them, but especially they learn how to teach others to use them.

Eighteen-Charlies are the engineers and learn all there is to know about building bunkers, field fortifications, bridges, towers, and other structures, and then how to take them apart again with explosives. Demolitions are a major subject area for the Charlies and they get lots of practice with C4, TNT, military dynamite, det cord, field expedient explosives, and the many ways to make these blasting agents detonate.

Medics—the 18-Deltas—spend over a year in training. During this time they learn how to treat disease and injuries both in people and animals. They learn how to diagnose illnesses and when to use antibiotics and other medications. All of them can perform surgery. In remote locations, the SF medic has all the responsibilities and most of the capabilities

of any physician, and in combat has to be ready to perform amputations and other emergency medical procedures.

Commo specialists—18 Echos—are sent to a 24-week program of intense study of radio systems. All SF commo sergeants can send Morse code, build many kinds of antennae, knows all the practical details of using UHF, VHF, satellite, secure, FM, AM radios—U.S. and foreign, new and old. Part of the training prepares these soldiers to set up and operate commo systems deep in hostile areas, or within tactical operations areas, especially now the satellite systems that let you chat with the Secretary of Defense—or rather, let him chat with you, while you are snuggled deep inside a hide site in a bad neighborhood.

Finally there is the 180A, a slot for a warrant officer. This career management field replaces a position that used to be held by a commissioned officer, the executive officer's role of a detachment, in the past assigned to a first lieutenant. Applicants for this position are already career Special Forces soldiers with at least three years experience in one of the NCO specialties, and must also be at least an E6 staff sergeant. They attend a SF Operations and Intelligence course and other training that, along with their previous experience, qualifies each to run a team.

So far each Special Forces student has been working on his individual skills, first the generic techniques, then the specialties, but never really being tested on the application of those skills as part of a team. That happens in the final part of the training for apprentice Green Berets. Over the course of 19 days, students are formed into standard Alpha detachments of 12 men, assigned a mission, briefed, equipped, and launched into the mythical nation of Pineland. Here they not only have to use all their specific skills but have to work with some very crabby guerrillas while being hunted by a well-armed OPFOR. The whole thing is a tremendous challenge for the students, an opportunity to pull it all together in something that resembles the challenges of the real unconventional world. At the end of the Robin Sage exercise, successful students will have finally earned the right to wear the green beret and Special Forces tab.

CHAPTER 2 **Armor**

Chapter 2 Armor

The Army fights in several fundamental ways. The infantry is one of these, in all its permutations—the light fighters, with all their virtues and vices. On the other end of the spectrum are the armored units with their main battle tanks and supporting combat vehicles.

These "heavy" divisions are heavy in every way—comprised of large numbers of complicated and expensive weapons, capable of massive destruction, with a logistics tail to match. As proven in the 1991 Gulf War, these people, weapons, support systems, and doctrine can work nearly flawlessly—once they are transported to the battlefield and prepared for combat, a process that took six months and the best efforts of the U.S. Air Force, U.S. Navy, and a lot of contract merchant vessels.

It is convenient to focus only on the tanks when discussing armored units, but (like in most of the rest of the Army's story) all sorts of people and systems are involved. Armored units operate as "task forces," temporary teams assembled by the commander to suit what he's got available and what sort of mission is being accomplished. Normally, when you see a platoon of M1 Abrams main battle tanks scurrying around in the desert, shooting up the place, there will be an M109 Paladin self-propelled howitzer battery somewhere nearby, protecting the tanks with indirect fire. M2 and M3 Bradley fighting vehicles will be prowling the flanks, scouting for enemy dismounts and missile teams and routes for the advance. M88 recovery vehicles will be close behind the advance, ready to rescue any tank or other vehicle that blows an engine. Further back will be an endless convoy of HEMTTs (Heavy Expanded Mobility Tactical Truck) and

5-ton trucks laden with fuel for all the vehicles, ammunition in every caliber, barrier material for the engineers, drinking water and MREs—everything needed to sustain the fight. Farther back will be the long-range weapons—the Multiple Launch Rocket System (MLRS) that can saturate an enemy position with a hailstorm of small sub-munitions, hitting it from 20 miles away. All of these weapons and the people who operate them are part of an armored division and an armored assault; neither one would work without them functioning as a team.

But there are big changes in this community right now. The tanks are successful when they finally arrive in the combat zone, but current Army transformation efforts are putting the heavy divisions on a weight-loss program. Right now, the Army can put a light force anywhere in the world within just a few days, and such a force can fight for a few days, but only that, with what they bring with them. Operation Desert Storm's long lead time was one of those lucky breaks—and combat commanders can't trust to luck very often and live.

Currently, following a strategy established by General Eric Shinseki, Army Chief of Staff from 1999, the Army is working on something called the Interim Force and planning its sequel, the Objective Force. Resources are being sucked out of the heavy divisions and used to build medium-weight light armored brigades. Fort Lewis, Washington, has traditionally been home to such schemes, and the 2nd Infantry Division, based there, was once known throughout the Army as the "Toys-R-Us" Division because of all the experimental weapons, vehicles, and other systems tested there. The 2nd ID is once again leading the charge, this time with its 3rd Brigade trading in its M1A2 Abrams tanks for the experimental Stryker vehicle. The 1st Brigade of the 25th ID is doing the same, with other units scheduled to follow …maybe.

The NTC Story

Tucked into a little corner of the great Mojave Desert, in a part of California that is nearly deserted, is a modern miracle, the National Training Center, called by everybody "NTC." During World War II, armored units trained here, a place where battalions and brigades of vehicles could work out the kinks of mobile warfare without worrying too much about annoying the neighbors with dust, smoke, noise, or the occasional stray cannon projectile. Known then and formally now as Fort Irwin, the post was desolate and deserted until a visionary Armor officer named Donn Starry and a few others began building a program to train the Army's tankers to fight and win against the Red Hordes of the Warsaw Pact.

General Starry was, at the beginning of the 1980s, boss of TRADOC, the Army's Training and Doctrine Command, the place where Pentagon policy gets converted to the tactics and techniques used to fight and win battles. Starry & Company helped revolutionize the Army's vision of ground combat, and the way soldiers prepared for ground combat.

They didn't know it at the time, but the incredible successes of the Army in "the great drive-by shoot-in" called the Gulf War were built directly on both the training and the doctrine invented by these few visionaries, of which NTC became one of the center-pieces.

They invented something called Air-Land Battle, and explained it in the Army's bible, *FM 100-5, Operations*, a book which described how armor, infantry, artillery, and aviation could all work together to defeat a much larger enemy. That was the theory, but the Army needed a big place to pull it all together. Fort Irwin provided the real estate, a thousand square miles of rough and ragged, sun-blasted desert with plenty of places to hide, plenty of places to run, and room enough to fire even 155mm cannon with "red bag" maximum charges.

This vast sandbox playground was just part of the story. About the same time, a technology was invented that used lasers to simulate the effect of direct-fire weapons like tank's main guns, machine guns, and rifles, a system called MILES. Using MILES provided a pretty good way to score accurately what actually happened when one weapon system fired at a target during tactical training. Before MILES, it was pretty much "bang-bang, you're dead." With MILES, a coded laser aligned with the weapon fired a beam of light every time the gun fired a blank round. Receivers on all the players in this game could tell when they were hit with a M16 round (not effective on a tank, disabling or fatal on a dismounted soldier) or a 120mm main gun round. Instead of depending on the veracity of the players, this system automatically shut down the weapon on the target when a killing shot was delivered. But the icing on the cake was the development of a huge computer system to keep score, relay transmitters on every hilltop, and a transmitter on every vehicle that reported back when weapons were fired and their effect. It became possible, for the first time, to know who really did what to whom out on the battlefield.

All this was a revolution for the Army, and would have been a success story even if Starry and his TRADOC subordinates (in and out of uniform) hadn't had one final brilliant inspiration: a professional, full-time set of bad guys. Designed to replicate the feared Red Horde, the NTC Opposing Force, or OPFOR was trained to use Warsaw Pact tanks, trucks, organization, and tactics. They even adopted black berets with bright red stars for headgear and fielded vehicles that looked like (and sometimes actually were) the T-72s, BRDMs, BMPs, and other systems the Army expected to see through its sights if NATO ever went to war with the Warsaw Pact forces.

The first units started coming to NTC in 1982, just in time to practice Air-Land Battle, and, as the Army likes to say, it was a "learning experience" for everybody. It took a while for the shock to sink in, for the word to get around the

Army, but the heavy units went through an ordeal that was entirely new. The OPFOR, with a home field advantage, overwhelming numbers, and troopers who became comfortable living in the field were formidable enemies. Commanders of heavy units from 3rd Armored Cav, the 2nd and 4th Infantry Divisions, and others finally had a chance to show their stuff against a brigade-sized opposing force, wring out their units, test gunnery and tactics, and let everybody operate in the field for three uninterrupted weeks. And, pretty much without exception, they had their proverbial clocks cleaned. The OPFOR, until now always defeated in maneuvers, started destroying the cream of the U.S. Army. One after another, confident, well-trained tank-infantry units were massacred by the rampaging Red Horde. It wasn't just that the tank units got shot up, but much worse—the OPFOR used Warsaw Pact doctrine and systems to jam communications, or play electronic warfare games with the visiting units. For years, the OPFOR could get on a Blue Force battalion radio net and issue orders that sent subordinate units to their doom. NTC quickly gained a reputation as a place where careers were made and lost, but mostly lost.

Part of the program was, and still is, a careful documentation of what happened in each battle, minute by minute, recorded by dozens of television cameras, sensors,

and ever-present observer-controllers (OCs). After each battle, the OCs led each unit through a "lessons learned" after-action review, showing what each did that worked and failed, with always an emphasis on success stories and the things that would make the next similar engagement more successful.

Instead of demoralizing these units, NTC spurred them and the rest of the Army to train realistically. And it all paid off in 1991 when these units went off to war against an army trained and equipped in classic Warsaw Pact style. The Iraqi Army was destroyed quickly and efficiently using the lessons learned in the Mojave. And, if you asked the tankers who killed all those T-72s, the real war wasn't as much of a challenge as an NTC rotation.

M1A2 Abrams

When first designed many years ago, and then fielded in 1980, the M1 Abrams was considered by many to be too expensive, too complicated and too radical. Its gas turbine engine, similar to those used on aircraft, was unique in a tank. Critics sneered at its fuel consumption, at the Abrams' composite "Chobham" armor, at its complex fire control system. Designed to go head-to-head with the Red Horde, the Abrams was intended to be a killing machine that could out-range Soviet adversaries, engage them through the dust and smoke of the battlefield before the enemy could fire back, and that could shrug off hits from the T-72s, T-64s, and T-55s that outnumbered NATO tanks by many times. Nobody thought the M1 would be invulnerable, but they thought each Abrams should be able to kill four or five or more of its adversaries before dying valiantly. As it turned out, both the critics and the advocates were both wrong— when the Abrams finally went to war, it literally "blew the doors off the competition." Hundreds of ex-Soviet main battle tanks—the very T-72s and T-55s it was designed to fight—were destroyed during the war in the Gulf, without the loss of a single Abrams to enemy fire.

The basic design has, like so many American systems today, been refined, enhanced, and up-graded rather than re-

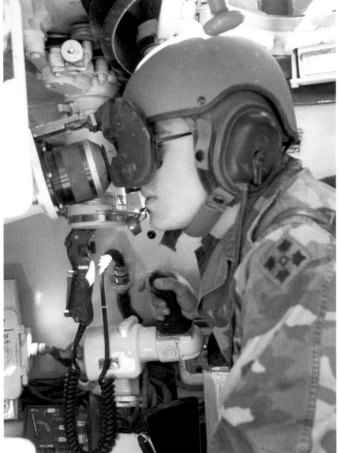

invented. The most advanced of these is currently the M1A2SEP, a 65-ton vehicle that is 26 feet long, 12 wide, and 8 feet high. Maximum rated speed is 45mph on roads, less on open ground. Four of these tanks form a platoon, with 14 in a typical company. In combat, tank platoons are "married up" with mech infantry platoons, usually two of one and one of the other—"tank-heavy" or "infantry-heavy," depending on the mission. These temporary units are called "teams."

Four men crew the Abrams, a driver (the entry-level job), loader, gunner, and commander (called the TC). Each platoon is commanded by an officer, normally a captain or first lieutenant. Each tank crew rehearses its skills till they are automatic, then the two-tank sections do the same, and then the platoons work together on their immediate action drills, how they will react to typical kinds of contact with enemy units, till all 16 guys can read each other's minds. The platoon leader needs a minimum of radio traffic to make things happen, an occasional hand and arm signal or the rare wave of a flag; mostly, each TC keeps an eye on the platoon leader's tank and follows the SOP.

The Abrams is a big vehicle but designed to minimize exposure to adversaries, most of whom can be expected to see it from the front. That's where the armor is heaviest, and where the gun is usually pointed. Early versions had a 105mm cannon, current M1A1s and A2s have a marvelously accurate 120mm smoothbore system. The lumpy thing on the tube is a fume extractor.

Within each tank, though, the crew communicate in a ritual way. Mostly, the TC tells them what to do and they comply without a word. "Driver, move out!" is how it begins, and the driver doesn't need to say a word, he takes his foot off the brake and applies pressure to the accelerator. Since the platoon moves together, as a formation, the driver knows where to put the vehicle. Only the platoon leader's driver needs any instruction, and even then, not much—it sounds like: "Driver, come right …follow the trail." The TC doesn't say anything unless something needs to be done differently.

Driving the Abrams is—superficially—easy, and fun. The transmission is automatic, the brake and gas pedals are in the normal places, you have a motorcycle-type steering control for changing direction. Put the transmission in drive, step on the gas, point it where you want to go. Acceleration is slower than with a car but the brakes are terrific. And, from a stop, you can put the transmission in P for "pivot," and then turn the whole vehicle on its vertical axis—perfect for parking in those tight spots. In reality it's not quite that simple. Tactical driving is in fact something of a minor military art. Moving smoothly at speed across desert, and not crashing into a big rock or wadi requires more skill than staying alive on a Los Angeles freeway.

The loader's position is on the left side of the turret, beside the TC. Ordinarily, when the unit is conducting a "traveling overwatch" or "movement to contact," the TC and loader will have their hatches open and they both may stand half exposed in them for better visibility. This is dangerous in one way, safer in another. The danger comes from an artillery airburst or a sniper. The safety comes from much better visibility and the ability to see threats, like enemy armor or anti-armor teams. The loader will man the 7.62 machine gun, useful against enemy dismounts and any enemy aircraft foolish enough to come within 500 meters or so.

In a combat zone, the TC will "battle-carry" a round in the gun, ready to fire immediately if the enemy is encountered. There are two choices, HE (high-explosive) or sabot. The HE round is effective against many kinds of targets, especially light armor and thin-skinned vehicles, but is not guaranteed to kill an enemy tank. The sabot is a long, thin, very heavy rod and can be made of "depleted" or non-radioactive uranium. This rod is much smaller than the bore of the gun, about 35mm in diameter in the 120mm bore, and is like a large dart. When fired, it leaves the muzzle traveling about 5,500 feet per second; the result is tremendous retained energy. The sabot round will reliably slice through any production tank's armor on the first shot, at ranges to three kilometers, and sometimes will keep going right through the other side, but whether it does or not it normally causes ammunition inside the target vehicle to

detonate. When fired at a truck or other "thin-skinned" enemy vehicle, though, the result is sometimes just a couple of holes in the sheet metal and nothing more.

The gunner and TC scan constantly for targets, each with a sector of responsibility. The TC takes from about the 9 o'clock position to about the 3 o'clock position, the gunner from around 10 to 2. Each has sights with selectable magnification and sensors, stabilized against vibration. A laser rangefinder will, at the push of a button, measure the distance to a target with great precision. The current SEP version of the Abrams provides the TC with the ability to search for, identify, and designate targets while the gunner is engaging a different target. When the first one is destroyed, the second can be engaged automatically—the gun tube slews around, aligns on the target, and is ready to fire as soon as the loader has fed a new round into the breach.

All this takes a lot more time to describe than actually to happen. Here's how it sounds in the turret:

"Gunner, sabot, tank!" calls the TC at the same time he points the tube at the target. The gunner sees the target, and calls,

"Identified!" He fine-tunes the alignment of the gun with his control (called a "Cadillac") and "lazes" the target to get the range. A fire control computer has already been set for the type of round, propellant temperature, wind speed and velocity, barometric pressure, the microscopic warp of the gun tube from the heat of the sun overhead, and the cant of the vehicle from level. The gunner puts the "cross-hairs" on the center of mass of the target, but the computer offsets the actual alignment based on all the ballistic variables.

In the second or two required for the gunner to react to the TC's warning order, the loader uses his right knee to operate a switch that controls the doors protecting the ammunition storage bins at the rear of the turret. He hits the base of a sabot round with his fist and it pops partway out of its rack. Deftly, he pulls the heavy round out, flips it end for end, feeds it into the breech, and rams it home in the chamber—not a job for weaklings! The breech block slams shut under spring tension, and the loader calls, "Up!"

Unless the TC has specified, "At my command," the gunner is cleared to engage and does so as quickly as possible, consistent with a good sight picture. He calls, "On the way!" and as he pronounces the "Y" in the word "way," squeezes the trigger on his Cadillac.

The noise inside the turret is rather mild. The gun recoils about two feet or so, then returns to battery. The Abrams lurches a bit. The gunner's and TC's view of the target is momentarily obscured by the propellant gasses, then it comes back into view in time to see the tracer element streak unerringly into the center of the enemy tank. In combat, impact is typically followed immediately by a flash as ammunition and fuel in the enemy tank ignite. If the target's

The latest evolution of the Abrams is the M1A2 SEP model incorporating improved FBCB2 digital communications and an automated fire control system that allows the commander to designate and hand-off targets to the gunner automatically.

INSET: *Despite all the new digital technology and sensor systems, the traditional Mk One Eyeball remains a critical part of the resources for tankers. Sgt. Gordon Tom watches enemy vehicles approach through the Valley of Death at the National Training Center.*

hatches are open, the pressure will vent through them. Buttoned up, the whole turret will probably be blown off and will fly several meters from the destroyed hull. Any crew inside will die an instant death. From start to finish, the whole process may last three to five seconds.

Bradley

While the Abrams and its crew fight primarily other tanks and tankers, the M2 and M3 Bradley Armored Fighting Vehicles stay nearby, ready to take on thinner-skinned adversaries, both mechanical and human. While the two versions of the Bradley appear outwardly similar, they are set up for rather different battlefield missions. The M2 is a "battlefield taxi," transporting seven combat-equipped soldiers under the protection of armor, turning them loose to clear bunkers, trenches, and enemy fighting positions otherwise impervious to direct-fire weapons. The M2 can also engage enemy tanks and defeat them with TOW (tube-launched, optically-tracked, wire-guided) missiles, but they don't try to make a habit of this. The TOW will outrange a tank main gun, but it is painfully slow and during the ten seconds or so that the missile flies toward its target, the Bradley is essentially nailed to the ground and vulnerable. The M3 is nearly the same vehicle but with more TOWs and room for one three-man team of dismounts—scouts,

perhaps, or a Javelin missile team to be bussed close to a hide site.

Both the M2 and M3 are armed with the M242 Bushmaster 25mm Chain Gun, a kind of machine gun on steroids. The Bushmaster is electrically driven and has two feed systems, each delivering its own specialized type of ammunition from bins below the gun, one with high explosive projectiles, the other with sabot rounds. This weapon will tear apart light armored vehicles like BMPs and BRDMs, and when the HE rounds impact an enemy truck, pieces of scrap metal fly everywhere. HE rounds will chew apart an enemy bunker, pillbox, or masonry structure. It is very effective against artillery systems, missile launchers, command and control vehicles, communications and radar vans, and especially fuel trucks. The sabot rounds are not as

RIGHT: *M2 Bradley's 25mm chain gun can't kill tanks but is very effective at killing almost anything else, including other AFVs. Two types of ammunition, sabot and HE, can be selected and automatically loaded during engagements.*

BELOW: *Often confused as a tank by most civilians, the M2 Bradley is actually a different breed of vehicle, with thinner armor, smaller gun, and different missions. Properly called an Armored Fighting Vehicle, its typical assignment is to team up with tanks and engaging enemy trucks and light armor vehicles.*

ABOVE: *Bradleys are fast, agile, and their TOW missiles can out-range and kill enemy main battle tanks, but when the enemy armor gets closer, it is time to go.*

LEFT: *Capt. Pete Fedak commands the headquarters company of 2nd Battalion, 8th Infantry, 4th Infantry Division – but you can just call it "two-eight" like everybody else. Two Eight is a "mech infantry" unit, accustomed to working with tanks in "task forces" custom designed for specific tactical problems.*

dramatic when they hit enemy armored fighting vehicles, but the projectiles slice through the aluminum armor generally found on such targets, putting them out of action.

The Bradley's gun system is quite sophisticated; the fire control equipment can automatically lock onto a target and track it as both the enemy vehicle and the Bradley scoot and scurry around the battlefield. As with the Abrams, the TC can designate one target while the gunner is engaging another; when the first is destroyed, the second is automatically presented to the gunner to be serviced.

Stryker

The Stryker, or LAV III, is a light armored vehicle with several versions that is currently part of a transformation of the Army. General Shinseki's idea was to convert six Abrams and Bradley brigades from the 2nd ID and 25th ID, replacing the heavier vehicles with faster, lighter, more-easily deployed Strykers as part of a much more mobile force. The scheme isn't quite working as advertised at this writing, but the idea might stick. Until then, the Army is gritting its teeth and soldiering on with the new vehicle.

It's actually a pretty well tested idea and a proven design. The LAV III is a Canadian vehicle with modifications for U.S. Army requirements, and the Army is planning on ten variants, some of which seem awfully dubious to old soldiers; even so, there's a lot to like about the design. Using eight large, "run-flat" tires, Stryker is very fast on any kind of road and still speedy over broken terrain. It will hold more soldiers than a Bradley—nine—but not as many as the ancient M113, which can carry a full squad of eleven. It's complicated, with a remote weapon station that (when it works, and it hasn't been working in tests) fires either a .50-caliber M2 heavy machine gun or a Mk 19 grenade launcher. For a "light vehicle," it is pretty heavy at about 40,000 pounds, much more than the M113's 27,200 pounds.

At this writing, Stryker variants all are too heavy for deployment on C-130s, one of the major selling points for the replacement of the Abrams. Strykers are too wide, also,

RIGHT: *According to some, this is the vehicle of the future, a lighter, faster, even more agile platform for the wars of the next decade and beyond, the Stryker.*

OPPOSITE, ABOVE: *Based on a Canadian design, the Stryker has very good performance on roads and across country. Early development examples, like this one going through trials at Fort Lewis, Washington, haven't quite lived up to all expectations – but that was true of the Abrams and Bradley, too, when first issued.*

OPPOSITE, BELOW: *Strikers have the new FBCB2 digital communications tactical internet and an automatic gun system, both of which still have a few bugs to be worked out.*

unless some components are dismounted. Soldiers are particularly worried about the mobile gun variant with its 105mm cannon and auto-loading system, currently way over weight at 41,000 pounds and at risk of roll-over when the gun is fired under some terrain conditions and gun angles. The armor that is supposed to be certified as safe against .50-caliber heavy machine gun fire may not be so safe after all, and certainly won't defeat the RPG-7 anti-armor weapon readily available to most likely enemies.

But the speed, nav and comms systems, cross country agility, and deployabilty might make it a success some day. If you stuff it full of troops and their gear, they'll all still be miserable—but they'll get where they're going faster, and that's okay. The traditionalists are in an uproar, and with some good reasons, but they were in an uproar, too, when the cavalry traded in their horses for Jeeps. The idea of a medium-weight force that fits between the instantly deployable Rangers and 82nd Airborne and the heavy Abrams divisions makes a lot of sense and will some day be a reality. Stryker, however, might not be the vehicle that is selected for the job.

M113 Armored Personnel Carrier and Variants

Anybody who thinks the military is always spending money on new weapons systems hasn't been riding around in the back of an APC recently. The first entered service in 1960 and more than 80,000 have been built since. It is a simple, slab-sided, vehicle, a kind of shoe box on tracks. Half-inch aluminum alloy armor is used throughout, giving minimal protection against small arms and artillery air bursts. A full-width ramp at the back allows passengers to depart and return quickly, and there's enough room inside for many kinds of cargo. In American service, the M113 isn't much used any more in its original "battlefield taxi" role, the Bradley having assumed that chore. Instead, the basic vehicle is always found stuffed full of radios and the other gear

ABOVE RIGHT: *M113 armored personnel carriers go back almost a half century and may be around for another fifty years. Here an observer-controller uses his "god gun" to kill an M1A2 Abrams during an exercise after an especially foolish tactical blunder. The god gun fires a coded laser that will shut down the Abrams until re-keyed.*

RIGHT AND OPPOSITE, ABOVE: *Although M113s are too slow and too lightly armored to get close to serious fighting, they are used extensively as the foundation for the Tactical Operations Centers (TOC) that are the mobile headquarters for fighting units. Inside will be found racks of radios and computers and the teams of people who coordinate artillery support, supply, aviation support, and all the operational planners who, under the commander's direction, make things happen.*

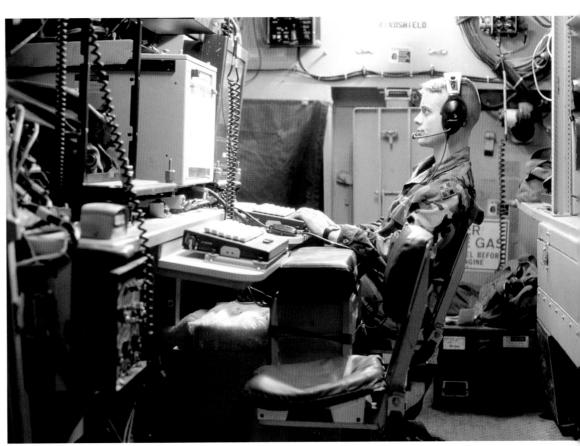

needed by the command staff, normally in a variant designated the M577. APCs have a distinctive sound as their tracks rattle and whine down the tank trails of the world, and it is unlikely that they will be retired entirely until well after half a century of service to the Army.

Unsung Heroes: The Battle Captain and the TOC

So much of modern American combat operations involves information processing. It has always been the foundation of successful combat command, but never more than the present. That's because things happen faster now, with smaller windows of tactical opportunity. To exploit those fleeting opportunities, a commander has to know what important things are happening, where, when, and how. He has scouts on the ground and in the air, electronic warfare specialists eavesdropping on the enemy, Joint Strike Attack and Radar System (JSTARS) aircraft and satellites overhead watching enemy movements on the ground, remotely piloted drones patrolling and sending back video, plus dozens of other resources, all feeding information back to the commander. If it were not for his Battle Captain and all the "staff pukes" in the Tactical Operations Center (TOC), he would drown in it.

The TOC is the commander's headquarters in the field, the place where the coffee is always hot and somebody is always awake. At the battalion level, a dozen people are usually on duty around the clock, and at critical times the place is stuffed with people, each busy in some specialized way. The FSO (Fire Support Officer, the guy in charge of artillery, subordinate to the operational commander) works out of here, always ready to send fire missions to the battery. The logistics officer, operations officer, intel officer, ADA, engineer officer, and the rest each have a little office here. They provide information to the commander, and get their orders from him in turn. Those offices are normally in an M577 parked cheek-by-jowl with others of its kind, and all covered by cammo nets.

RIGHT: *NTC's OPFOR are masters of writing and presenting operational orders, or "op orders," the briefing that preceeds deliberate combat operations. Here, the staff is building a huge terrain map in intricate detail as an aid to explain how the battle should be fought tomorrow. Under camoflage nets at the top of the hill is the regiment's TOC.*

INSET: *Day or night, somebody is always listening to the radios and the coffee is always hot in the TOC. Just before the issue of op orders, the place is full to overflowing with officers and NCOs all working hard to finish one part of the big plan.*

The commander doesn't try to manage this potential bedlam—he has other things to do, one of which is to talk to his boss at the brigade or division TOC. As his representative—an office manager, if you like—is one officer who keeps it all under control, the Battle Captain. Normally a trusted and senior captain who has previously commanded a company in the same battalion, this officer decides how to deal with all the routine events and when to wake up the boss. He or she (and women are often present in most TOCs) has been called the supervisor of a crisis management center, and that's not a bad description.

What happens when an observation post detects movement through their LRASSS (Long Range Advance Scout Surveillance System) at 0200, or scouts report isolated bursts of machine-gun fire in their sector? What does a dust cloud 20 kilometers to the front signify? Signal flares? Illumination rounds fired near a friendly formation or an obstacle? The battle captain's duty is to verify the information first, evaluate it second, and pass it along to the commander if it has significance for his plan. The TOC is an interesting, important, place filled with people to match. And it is one of the first targets for enemy forces, if they can find it and reach it.

LEFT: *M88 recovery vehicles and their crews can pull an Abrams or Bradley out of the mud, quickly swap an engine or transmission, or replace a track.*

BELOW LEFT: *Sometimes an armored unit needs the help of brave dismounts like this combat engineer with a bangalore torpedo – a piece of pipe full of explosive, in this case, primed and fused and ready to place. Engineers breach enemy wire obstacles this way, and have other skills to keep the advance from being channeled into enemy kill zones.*

RIGHT: *An ACE, or Armored Combat Earthmover, digs a fighting postion for the M1 Abrams tank waiting in the background. Such positions allow the tank to hide while the enemy advances, only coming out of the hole long enough to get off a shot, then disappearing again.*

NEXT PAGE: *After the battle, late on a night with a clear sky and full moon, NTC's OPFOR reconstitute and tell war stories around campfires.*

INSET LEFT: *Within the TOC, one officer keeps control of all the information flowing in and out, the battle captain.*

INSET RIGHT: *At the end of the battle, in training and in war, soldiers conduct an AAR, – after action review.*

CHAPTER 3 Eleven Bravo – Infantry

Chapter 3 Eleven Bravo – Infantry

Overview

Regardless of all the "high-speed/low-drag" battery-powered systems purchased at great expense by the Department of Defense, the Army and Marine Corps both insist that there is no alternative for the guy on the ground with a rifle, an attitude and a mission, and this premise still appears to be true. Smart bombs have worked wonders in Afghanistan and elsewhere, but only when a guy on the ground with a laser-designator could point out the target. These soldiers on the ground have been doing what was previously considered impossible—defeating highly skilled, well-armed, battle-tested Afghan irregulars on their home field, at their own game, despite the predictions of disaster by legions of observers.

There is nothing common about the Army's foot soldier today, although he shares a lot of characteristics with infantry of the past. Although adept at long foot marches, the modern infantryman is likely to ride most of the way to his operational area, in a helicopter or an M2 Bradley or under a T-10 parachute. Once on the ground, in range of the enemy, Eleven Bravos conduct business pretty much the same way as always. That business is based on teams that are organized and equipped for specialized missions, each in tiny building blocks, and each team supporting a larger team. For example, three men form a fire team, with four fire teams in a squad. Four squads make up a platoon and four platoons build a company. Within each company will be some riflemen, some soldiers with missiles, some grenadiers, some mortar-men, some radio operators (RTOs).

All the men in an infantry platoon are infantry soldiers, but with several specialties. The 11B rifleman is the core and foundation of it all. Even at the entry level, the rifleman has a skilled job that can at times be quite technical. He is executes his role in combat operations somewhat like a member of a football team, blocking or running, attacking or defending based on a scripted, rehearsed, complex performance directed by his coach, the fire team leader, or squad leader, or platoon leader. A journeyman 11B is adept with rifle or carbine, of course, but can also call for artillery support, build fighting positions, and deliver first aid to major trauma cases.

Mech Infantry

While all the light fighters in the Airborne, Air Assault, Mountain, and similar units get all smug about how miserable they like to be, the mechanized infantry don't care; they ride to work in safety and comfort, sleep in the wonderful new sleeping bags instead of wrapped in a poncho liner in the mud, and, when the poop hits the propeller, they usually have some heavy firepower nearby to clean house.

After a long period of neglect, Egyptian forces fighting Israeli tanks in the Sinai Desert during the 1973 war powerfully confirmed the role of infantry in support of armor. Briefly, foolishly, the Israeli army sent its tanks into battle "pure," without supporting infantry. The APCs that carried the soldiers were slower than the tanks, and much more vulnerable to anti-armor weapons. Near the Suez canal, Israeli tanks got mixed up with Egyptian soldiers equipped with Russian Sagger missiles in a battle that wasn't supposed to happen.

The Sagger is a little wire-guided missile that is carried in what looks like a small suitcase. It is easy to set up and can be fired by a soldier with very little training. A joystick controls the flight of the missile and when it hits a target, a shaped-charge warhead detonates, forming a jet of superheated gas that can blast a hole through quite a bit of conventional steel armor. The portability of the Sagger and its ease of employment should have worried the Israeli commanders, but it didn't—they didn't know about it until the missiles started flying from the tops of sand dunes and slamming into their tanks, knocking them out of action by the dozens. It was a rude shock, and unnecessary. But war involves taking chances and calculating risks, and sometimes loosing a bet.

Tanks are great for fighting other tanks, and even better for fighting defenseless thin-skinned trucks and APCs, but terrible for defending against infantry with places to hide and with effective anti-tank weapons. So the Israelis quickly changed their plan, called for the APCs and infantry, and the troops started clearing the Egyptian missile teams. This was

RIGHT: *"What are you doing here?" Lt. Col. Ricardo Riera asks, prodding one of his company commanders to get his people moving. "You're supposed to be on the objective by now!" Battles are won by commanders like this one who know how to train subordinates before the shooting starts. Riera, like many of the officers and NCOs in 2nd Battalion, 8th Infantry Regiment, 4th Infantry Division, are Rangers with combat experience and gold stars on their jump wings. They lead the way.*

a lesson American (and, really, all) armies rediscovered as a result of the Yom Kippur War, and today you won't find many American tankers who are sent to battle except as part of a tank-infantry team.

The masters of this fine art form are probably the 4th Infantry Division based at Fort Hood, Texas. As an example of how it works, consider the 2nd Brigade, with its one infantry battalion (the 2nd Battalion of the 8th Infantry Regiment, but always referred to as either "Two-Eight" or "Second of the Eight"), and two tank battalions (1st of the 67th and 3rd of the 67th), plus one engineer battalion, the 588th. Now, most of the time, when the division is in garrison, the tankers and the infantry and the engineers all go off to secluded nooks and crannies of the vast post and train on their specialized skills all by themselves—in their "pure" organizations. The soldiers practice working with their own ("organic" is the term for assets owned by the unit) AFVs, M2A2 Bradleys, riding around inside and dashing out to assault pretend enemy positions. They clear bunkers and trenches, fire their TOW and Dragon missiles, shoot their M16s and M249 SAWs, work on movement techniques and immediate action drills. Think of all this as something like individual musicians maintaining proficiency with their instruments, and then gathering as groups—the horn section, say, or the strings in an orchestra—to practice with groups of similar specialists.

But in the real world of modern mech infantry and armored combat, these groups are cut and pasted together in "task forces" designed to accomplish specific missions. Some of these task forces might be "armor heavy" if the brigade is going up against an enemy tank unit, or it might be loaded with Bradleys and 11Bs. This is done by the brigade commander (who is not, as a rule, a brigadier but a colonel) who "chops" or assigns tank companies to work with infantry companies in custom-designed task forces.

As big and rugged as Fort Hood is, there really isn't room for brigades to do realistic training that replicates the real world. Instead, the 4th ID and all similar units frequently visit one of the Army's biggest and best success stories, the National Training Center (NTC).

"Leg" Infantry

These infantry units are seldom organized in combat the way they are in garrison. The combat commander and his subordinates "task-organize" the units that are sent into battle, mixing some people and assets from one group with members of another, depending on the specific mission. Such formations are called "task forces" and it is rare indeed that a battalion goes into battle "pure," with only its own personnel.

In Afghanistan, an infantry company might find itself with extra engineers who are artists with C4 explosive and "det" cord if the commander expects to find caves and bunkers full of enemy ammo. If Air Force close-air-support (CAS) is an important part of the plan, one or more USAF Forward Air Controllers (FACs) will likely be "chopped" to walk the ground with the infantry, always ready to call for help from on high.

Lessons Learned, and Re-learned

The success of the Army's foot soldiers—the "Eleven Bravos"—has been the result of lessons learned and applied during the last 20 years or so. The lessons were learned in the invasion of Grenada, Panama, and Iraq, then applied to training and doctrine at JRTC (the Joint Readiness Training Center), NTC (the National Training Center at Fort Irwin,

rucksacks have commonly weighed 120 pounds. Even Rangers have trouble moving with such loads for more than a short distance, on firm, level ground. When 11Bs try it in the high altitudes and rocky terrain of Afghanistan, these loads have been invitations to falls, broken bones, and exhaustion.

Light—10th Mountain

One of the star performers in recent real-world conflicts has been the "light fighters" of Fort Drumm, New York's, 10th Mountain Division. Like the 82nd Airborne and 101st Airborne, the 10th Mountain is an infantry formation of the old school, without a lot of organic artillery, armor, or the assets to fight for very long without support from other units. Its training has been tested in the Gulf, Somalia, Haiti, Bosnia and Afghanistan, and when al Queda prisoners rioted at the Qalai Janghi prison on 26 November 2001, it was 10th Mountain soldiers who were first in to the rescue of Special Forces and USAF personnel.

Like its World War II ancestors, its soldiers are prepared to walk long distances, fight at night, at high altitude, and in cold conditions. During Operation Enduring Freedom, units of the 10th set up a base in Uzbekistan on a former Soviet airfield, then mounted operations against the Taliban. Although its lack of armor and organic artillery makes it vulnerable to some kinds of enemy forces, the division's light weight makes it easy to move into and around the combat zone. Its massive fleet of Black Hawk and Chinook helicopters, night vision systems, and FBCB2 communications all give the 10th Mountain the ability to strike quickly and from unexpected directions.

What the Well-Dressed 11B Wears to Work

Soldier Systems Command is the organization within the Army that frets and fusses about what the soldier should be wearing—the basics as well as the fashion accessories. Everything from boots to helmet is their responsibility, along with all the stuff a soldier carries on his back, front, and sides.

You can spot somebody "out of the loop" when they write newspaper articles including the word "fatigues." Soldiers all wear BDUs, "battle dress uniforms," that have been standard issue for more than 20 years. They come in lightweight fabric for summer and a heavier material for cooler seasons, and in two basic camouflage patterns, "woodland," and "desert." BDUs are generally considered comfortable, durable, and well-designed for their function—unlike the old fatigues that were designed to look good, were frequently heavily starched, and tailored nearly skin tight. Very few soldiers of any rank "break starch" or spit-shine their boots anymore—instead, the BDUs are okay right out of the dryer and boots polished with a brush will

California), and everywhere else the Army rehearses. Instead of becoming irrelevant, the infantry has become irreplaceable. Soldiers from the 10th Mountain, 82nd Airborne, 101st Airborne (Air Assault), and especially from the Special Forces groups, have been getting "blooded" in Afghanistan, re-learning old lessons and inventing new ones. This is a new golden age for the infantry.

There's a catch phrase in the Army that goes, "We train the way we fight." It sounds good, but isn't true, as battalions of infantrymen have been discovering in Afghanistan. Infantry soldiers know that they can't fight well while burdened with heavy rucksacks, and during training there are strict limits on how much weight each man is permitted to carry. Every combat experience of the U.S. Army has proven that soldiers need to carry the bare minimum—ammunition first and foremost, because if you run out of that you stop fighting right away, water second, because if you run out of that you're going to be useless soon, batteries for radios and night vision goggles (NVGs), and everything else is pretty much optional. That's the way soldiers try to train, but every time they go off to combat, all those training lessons evaporate.

In Grenada, Panama, and Afghanistan, soldiers have been overburdened with double loads of ammunition, batteries, water, and "snivel gear" to the point where

pass most inspections. Soldiers refer to such preparation as "fluff and buff."

American soldiers still carry about the same combat load as their ancestors of the Civil or Revolutionary Wars, and often in pouches not all that different from the distant past. The standard system is called TA-50 or Load Bearing Equipment (LBE), and is nearly identical to the gear carried by the American infantry in World War II, with a heavy belt carrying canteens and first-aid pouch and ammunition and

sundries, but today's is made of nylon instead of cotton and doesn't rot.

This basic system has proven to have some virtues—it is easily adapted to the individual soldier's specialized gear and anatomy, carries the weight low and well distributed, and provides support from both the shoulders and hips. Ammunition pouches holding three 30-round M16 magazines each are normally attached to the front of the belt, with one or two canteens on the hips. A "blow-out patch," as the combat wound dressing is sometimes called, is always attached to the left suspender by Army-wide SOP so that, when you get shot, the first person to crawl over to you knows exactly where to go looking for the plug that will keep all your juices from leaking out. Infantry soldiers, particularly leaders, will often have a compass attached to the right suspender, and the belt may have attached a butt-pack, a gas mask carrier, a pouch for night vision goggles, and an M9 bayonet. Traditional LBE is light, comfortable if properly fitted, and allows good ventilation. It puts your magazines right at your fingertips. And, if you get shot, your

BELOW: *When first introduced back in the 1960s, the M60 machinegun quickly acquired a nickname – "the pig." It is heavy, greedy in its consumption of ammunition, and powerful. Although rated at the ability to fire about 600 rounds per minute, that's not the way you use it – methodical bursts of ten to 30 rounds, sweeping across your sector, then pausing to keep it from getting too hot. In heavy combat, when there is no choice, the barrel will glow red, the bore will burn out, and ammunition cooks off even if the trigger isn't being pulled.*

LEFT: *Lt. Col. Tim Wray, beloved commander of 3rd Battalion, 17th Infantry, 7th Infantry Division. Battalion commanders are evangelists, confessors, CEOs, visionaries. Tim Wray was a good one.*

BELOW LEFT: *Radio communication has been a growing part of tactical operations, although sometimes tactical leaders would like to turn the thing off (and sometimes do). New systems like GPS, FBCB2, SINCGARS, and Land Warrior, make it possible for battalion commanders to know where their companies are all the time – and to tell them what to do, too.*

PREVIOUS PAGE: *A company of infantry from the 82nd Airborne Division emerges from a smoke screen during a firepower demonstration at Fort Bragg's Sicily Drop Zone. Although their weapons and uniforms are different from those of the men of the 82nd during World War II, their mission and doctrine is pretty much the same – jump into an objective, seize it by shock, surprise, and maneuver, then hold on tight till follow-on forces arrive with the tanks and artillery.*

PREVIOUS PAGE, INSET: *An infantry company commander and his RTO (radio-telephone operator) pause momentarily to observe the route ahead. They are assaulting a bunker complex one kilometer ("click" in the vernacular) ahead, behind a hill. 155mm artillery rounds are impacting on the objective now, the artillery "prep" that should make the mission a bit easier. Both men have been up for about thirty six hours, have been moving all night, and haven't showered in a week. In a moment, they will move out, the company with them, and prepare for the final movement to the assault.*

buddies can grab the LBE harness behind the shoulders and drag your carcass out of the line of fire.

Some soldiers accessorize their LBE with a carabiner on the right and sometimes a Ranger pace counter. The pace counter is a kind of dehydrated abacus, just two sets of beads strung on some parachute suspension line (called "550 cord"), and is used during land navigation exercises to keep track of distance traveled. The carabiner is really a mountaineering and rock-climbing tool that started being used by Special Forces soldiers in Vietnam. Instead of standard LBE, these guys wore a kind of parachute harness over their uniform, adapted to carry ammo and canteens, and invented by a sergeant named McGuire. But when the enemy was closing in, while they were deep in the jungle and far from a pick-up zone, a UH-1B helicopter could come to a hover over their position, throw down prepared ropes, and the members of the team could snap a "beener" into a loop on the rope. When everybody was snapped in, and sometimes before, the helicopter could pull pitch, pull the team up and out of the jungle, and fly away home.

The technique is still practiced and many soldiers have had a ride on the end of those "strings," but that's not really why they have them on their LBE today. The carabiner is a handy place to stow your gloves, and you can run the sling of your M16 or M4 through it so it doesn't get lost—but, as one soldier told me when asked about his, "It looks really cool!"

Replacing the traditional harness over the past couple of decades is a completely different kind of load-bearing system, the assault vest. The very first such vests were adaptations of aircrew survival vests produced during the Vietnam War, and then M79 40mm grenadiers got a vest to hold their basic load of ammunition. Ranger riflemen started wearing a vest about 1980; Rangers like to shoot and so they go through more ammunition than almost anybody, and the vests (which, by the way, looked a lot like those worn by Chinese and Russian AK-47 riflemen) carried a lot of magazines.

The current assault vest is constructed mostly of nylon mesh, with snap closures at the front. It holds eight 30-round magazines, with additional stowage for grenades, rings for the blow-out patch, pace-counter, and all the same gear carried on the LBE. The very newest vest system doesn't have fixed pouches but a lattice of attachment points that permit the soldier to set up the vest to suit himself.

M16 Rifle

The Department of Defense has a reputation for constantly buying new weapons systems at great cost and great waste. This is rarely true, and no better example is the story of the soldier's individual weapon, the M16 rifle or M4 carbine. The basic weapon design that is carried by most Green Berets, Rangers, infantry, and other soldiers—as well as

LEFT: *A cold, damp December day at Fort Hood, Texas, brings out the "snivel gear," especially the ECWCS (Extreme Cold Weather Clothing System) Gortex™ jacket as worn by this 4th ID soldier. The Army's Soldier Systems Command has come up with some tremendous improvements on jackets, the ballistic helmet, sleeping bags, and related gear to keep the troops comfortable, and the light, warm, ECWCS jacket is just one of their recent success stories.*

BELOW LEFT: *At the other end of the climate spectrum, this soldier at NTC has been training in daytime ground temperatures that can exceed 130-degrees Fahrenheit. His BDUs (Battle Dress Uniform) is made of a lightweight, rip-stop material that is reinforced and double-layered at wear areas. The Kevlar helmet is reasonably comfortable (for a helmet) and has actually stopped bullets. Along with everything else, these soldiers wear MILES harnesses used to record hits by laser beams simulating enemy weapons.*

RIGHT: *What the well-dressed combat medic wears to work: standard ALICE rucksack with extra canteen, entrenching tool ("E-tool" to the troops), foam sleeping mat, and combat life-saver pack on top of the ruck. Those are night vision goggles (NVG) attached to the helmet, and don't lose them – you'll have to pay $7,000 to replace them, and the chain of command will still be very, very angry.*

Navy SEALs, Air Force, Marine Corps, Coast Guard, and personnel from many foreign nations—goes back more than half a century.

The story of the M16 begins in 1948 with a study at Johns Hopkins University exploring the lessons learned during World War II. Research and development work done in the 1950s produced a prototype weapon based on a modified Remington .222 sporting cartridge. This rifle was designed by Eugene Stoner and incorporated features already proven in other American and European weapons. Stoner, however, used aluminum alloy for the receiver and plastic for the stock in a rifle designated the AR-15.

Testing of the AR-15 began in 1958 and, despite howls of protest from many who favored the more traditional M14, it gradually gained favor. Adoption of any new device, especially one as important as a rifle, is a very political business, and in 1963 Colt finally began producing the weapon, now known as the M16 and officially adopted in 1964. There were teething problems with the weapon, with the ammunition, with the way the soldiers were trained to use and maintain it. We called it "the plastic rifle" when it first came out, but it looked so cool and "space-age" that most troopers were intrigued.

Today's M16 and M4 are not much different on the outside from their ancestor. In the rifle variant, today's M16A2 is a little longer and a little heavier than the version of 40 years ago, and instead of full-automatic fire (for "spray and pray" engagements), the A2 fires three-shot bursts besides single rounds.

It is a pleasant weapon to fire, with negligible recoil that makes it easy to evaluate the effect of your fire, and easy to re-acquire your target to re-engage. At only 8.3 pounds (3.77kg), you can carry it all day and all night, although, like any weapon, it is guaranteed to get heavier the longer you carry it. The weight saved in the weapon and the ammunition is substantial when compared with previous rifles, but that doesn't mean you carry less weight. You get to carry the same weight as any infantry soldier going back to the Roman legions or before, 70 pounds or more, but within that load is a lot more ammunition—it varies with the mission, the unit SOP, and sometimes personal preference, but too much is never enough when you are being fired on.

RIGHT: *A company of 7th ID light fighters move toward their objective like the professionals they are, ten meters apart, weapons oriented out, in "traveling overwatch." All infantry soldiers are accustomed to such road marches although the men of the Airborne/Air Assault, Mountain and Light divisions do more than any except perhaps Rangers.*

Rangers and other hardcore soldiers will go out the door with 300 or more rounds for their personal weapon, along with all the cross-loaded gear.

According to the official specs, you are supposed to be able to engage an area target (a group of enemy soldiers in the open, for example) effectively at 800 meters and point targets (an individual enemy soldier) at 550 meters, but whoever published those figures was an optimist. In combat, you're lucky to score a hit on an enemy soldier at 100 meters, even if he's standing still and holding a sign saying "shoot me!", something they seldom do. On the range, most soldiers can knock down targets out to 200 meters with fair reliability, and at 300 meters occasionally, but beyond that hits are few and far between.

The M16 and M4 carbine are great combat weapons, though, and have certainly killed a lot of bad guys. This is particularly true when used by Rangers and Special Forces soldiers who've fired tens of thousands of rounds through their weapons under all kinds of scenarios. Using the new PEQ-4 laser sight/illuminator, the M16 and M4 are highly effective, but even these soldiers seldom expect to engage enemy soldiers effectively outside 100 meters or so.

How to Eat an MRE

Almost any soldier in the U.S. Army, at least among those who go to the field, has to be ready to survive for days, weeks, or months on MREs, the legendary Meals, Ready to Eat, sometimes called "Meals, Rejected by Ethiopians." Despite sneers from members of the Navy and Air Force, who don't go to the field anyway, MREs are a huge success and gourmet fare (under the circumstances) if you are tired, cold, hungry, and far from civilization. Almost everybody likes at least some of the 24 menus, and with good reason— they are a great solution to the problem of feeding soldiers during field operations.

MREs started replacing Vietnam era C-rations ("C-rats" to an entire generation) in the 1980s. They come twelve to a case, each in a sturdy plastic pouch that just fits in your BDU pants cargo pocket. C-rats were pretty good but came in tin cans that could be heavy to carry and a bit awkward to open unless you had the little P-38 tool that most soldiers of that dim and distant time carried on their dog-tag chain. Cs were okay, for cold, canned food, if nothing else was available—and often, it wasn't.

Each MRE pouch has an entrée, crackers, something to spread on the crackers, some kind of sweet, and an accessory packet. If you actually ate everything in the package, chewed the gum, drank the cocoa and the "bug juice"—and nobody has ever actually been observed to do this—the whole meal is worth about 1300 calories. That's a lot of food for one meal and so most soldiers pick and choose, or save parts of one MRE for a snack or to combine with something else later. Your "first shirt" (as the company's first sergeant is

LEFT: *Rucksack contents: sleeping bag, poncho, spare underwear and socks, clothing, personal hygiene items, and more. Based on experience in Afghanistan, many soldiers are re-thinking all of this, and doing without almost everything visible in this photograph, including the sleeping bag even in rather cold conditions. Instead, the thinking goes, the soldier should carry only mission-essential equipment, and that is ammunition, batteries, and water. Everything else is a luxury. And when you already have eighty pounds of ammo, batteries, and water in the ruck, you really shouldn't be carrying any more weight.*

OPPOSITE, ABOVE: *Company commander, 82nd Airborne Division.*

OPPOSITE, BELOW: *Many soldiers attach a carabineer or snap-link to their LBE (load bearing equipment). Originally used for clipping a "Swiss seat" into a rappelling rope or for extraction from jungle by helicopter, the device is now used as a handy attachment point for gloves, spent magazines (if they have been "tabbed" with a loop of "dummy cord") and other such items. But as one soldier said, when asked what it was for, replied, "Nothing much – I just think it looks cool!"*

usually called) or some other NCO will show up with a truck-load of MRE cases first thing in the morning; if you're getting hot chow, this is your chance to grab something for lunch; if you aren't getting hot chow, you'll take two or three pouches to get you through the day. Most soldiers have favorites and paw through the boxes looking for the best ones, or MREs they haven't already eaten 20 times in the past two weeks. Latecomers will get the vegetarian bean burrito.

Each MRE now comes with its own little heater, activated by water, a wonderful addition. All you do is open the heater pouch, slip in the entrée pouch, add a little bit of water, and wait about 15 minutes. Not only does this heater heat the food, it can heat you at the same time if you're freezing in some desolate hole on a mountain in Afghanistan or, even colder, out on OP 11 at Fort Bragg in January. The team who came up with this heater has the gratitude of modern field soldiers—especially the few still around who remember trying to heat those old C-rats.

The meals themselves are good, and the Army's Soldier Systems Command has been doing a great job of coming up with new and improved ones while getting rid of unpopular ones. If you get first shot at a typical case, options you can chose from include chili and macaroni, ham slice, beef frankfurters, pork chow mein, meat loaf, chicken with noodles, chicken stew, beef stew, chicken and rice and, for vegetarians, cheese tortellini and pasta with vegetables. Actually, you can find people who love or hate any of them. It is common for soldiers from a unit to trade components back and forth, a pound cake for chocolate nut bar, for example, or the bean burritos for chicken and rice.

Here are some comments from the field:

"Though I am not a vegetarian, my favorites are the vegetarian ones, most with pasta. I can remember a deployment to Egypt when the 1SG had to limit them to true vegetarians since they were so popular. Hard to say what the worst is, but for me if I only get jelly versus

RIGHT: *Capt. Reggie Salazar, commander of the headquarters company of 2nd Battalion, 8th Infantry, 4th Infantry Division, a mechanized infantry unit. He's equipped with an M4 carbine, a compact version of the M16 rifle that is issued to many soldiers in and out of the special operations community. The scope works with his NVG. The PEQ-4 laser illuminator attached to the front of the forward grip can be used to designate targets, engage them, and can also be used like a broad-beam flashlight that can only be seen with night vision systems.*

INSET: *Hot chow and fresh fruit in the field doesn't happen too often, especially when units are moving fast or are forward-deployed, but the cooks work through the night, then truck the chow long distances in insulated containers to the training areas. It is always a welcome change from the MREs, especially when accompanied by fresh, cold milk.*

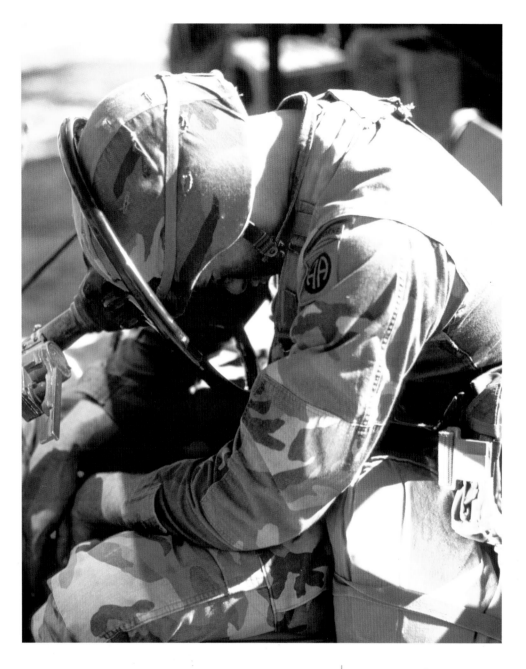

LEFT: *This 82nd Airborne trooper has been going for forty eight hours non-stop…well, he's stopped now. Army leaders know how essential a sleep plan is, and officers and NCOs try to make sure everybody gets at least some sleep every day, even if it is just a series of catnaps. Our hero slept this way for no more than five minutes before his commander returned; awoke instantly, started the engine and drove off.*

BELOW LEFT: *"Hummers" or "humvees" (officially, High Mobility Multipurpose Wheeled Vehicle") come in many variants, for many purposes. This one mounts a TOW (Tube-launched, Optically tracked, Wire-guided) missile and is standard issue for scouts like the ones employing it here. Although the missile will kill enemy armor up to three kilometers away, scouts know better than to fight with tanks; it is a last-ditch self defense weapon that might rarely be useful for a cheap shot at an isolated target. This vehicle has an armor kit installed that will resist small arms fire, some artillery fragments, and not much more.*

ABOVE RIGHT: *Combat engineers assault toward their objective, a bunker complex 300 meters to the right, already on fire from artillery high explosive hits. They have the dangerous and difficult mission of breaching the enemy's wire and mines, opening the door to the position through which the infantry will run before clearing the bunkers and trenches.*

RIGHT: *Soldiers now routinely train with body armor that protects against one kind of danger while at the same time creating another, heat stress. This soldier was a borderline heat casualty, a result of too much running in 90-degree heat, high humidity, while wearing a flak jacket, and carrying weapon and equipment. The medic, always looking for an excuse to stick somebody, decided to give him an IV for practice.*

peanut butter or cheese, it is gonna be a rough day. The best insert is probably the jalapeño cheese spread."

One of the brilliant things SSC did with MREs was adding a tiny bottle of Tabasco sauce to each package, just like the standard bottle available in any American store, but much smaller. This allows you to perk up just about anything, adding a little variety to your meals. And variety is the problem with MREs, even with 24 menus. Almost everybody adores the Tabasco sauce.

After a while, the similarity of it all tends to drive people to desperate measures. It all begins by fortifying the cocoa with the sugar packet and the dry creamer—this is a good and ancient trick taught me at a very remote Special Forces outpost in Vietnam in 1962, and tastes exactly the same today as back then. And you can make a sandwich with the crackers and the meatloaf or ham slice, although it is going to be messy because the crackers are very brittle. Some MREs now have bread instead of crackers, and it is pretty good, especially for making sandwiches. But if you're really stuck out there, with not even a T-rat ("tray-ration," or t-rat, a field nutrition package for feeding groups of soldiers in the field) for special occasions, it won't be long till you're mixing the cheese spread with the Mexican rice, or inventing casseroles by cutting up bits of ham or beef and adding them to the chicken stew, and trying every other possible combination.

"Ranger Pudding" is made several ways, as Captain Pete Fedak reported in an earlier chapter and MRE mocha (add three instant coffee packets to the cocoa, creamer and sugar packets) isn't bad. But whatever you do, how desperate you are, don't try putting the Tabasco sauce in the coffee or cocoa—it doesn't work, trust me on this. There is one sure way to tell somebody has been out in the field too long and it is time to send him in—when he starts making "MRE Jambalaya," (everything in the MRE package, including the gum, coffee, bug juice, Tootsie Roll, and chewing gum, all in one ghastly mélange) and claiming to like it. When you start doing that, you're a combat casualty and it's time to call for the medics.

LEFT: *Although American soldiers don't like to fight from fixed positions and trenches unless they have to, all units learn to deal with this kind of tactical problem by experience and practice.*

ABOVE: *Dragon is an anti-armor missile that can defeat main battle tanks from the sides or rear, and sometimes even from the front. They make a huge amount of noise and a large flash when launched, but all you have to do to score a hit is to keep the sight aligned on the target center-of-mass during the ten seconds required for the missile to get down range.*

RIGHT: *An M18 Claymore anti-personnel mine, with its blasting cap, firing device, continuity tester, and . Inside the plastic case is a sheet of C-4 plastic explosive in which are embedded 700 steel balls. When fired, its kill zone is a sixty-degree fan out to fifty meters, and can produce casualties out to 250 meters.*

OPPOSITE: *Belted ammunition ready for issue in the field. Machinegun ammunition typically is belted up with four "ball" projectiles for each tracer round, color coded orange. A small bit of phosphorus in a well at the base of the bullet is ignited when the round is fired and burns bright red for about one second, easily permitting the gunner to evaluate the impact of his burst.*

OPPOSITE, INSET: *M240 7.62mm machinegun. This Belgian weapon designed by Fabrique Nationale Manufacturing, Inc., and has been selected to replace the old M60. The M240 has been found to be more durable, reliable, and easier to maintain – but no easier to carry than the old "pig." It weighs about 25 pounds unloaded.*

NEXT PAGE: *Parades and review are impressive to watch but dreary dull events for those in the back of the ranks. These reviews, like the bayonets on the rifles of these soldiers, both are echoes of the ancient traditions of the profession of arms. These soldiers are at parade rest, with weapons at the sling arms position.*

LEFT: *Mortars are the last vestige of muzzle-loading smoothbore cannon, and this M224 60mm is a prime example. Found in Ranger, Airborne, and light infantry units across the Army, it can move with the assault element and provide a kind and volume of accuate fire not provided by any other weapon. Every man in an infantry unit in combat is normally carrying one or two rounds for the M224. In extremis, the crew can fire thirty rounds per minute, either by dropping them down the bore or with the trigger, just visible at the base. Each round comes with its fuse installed and additional propellant increments attached to the fins. Complete, this little mortar weighs about forty-five pounds, too much for one man to routinely carry in addition to his normal load, so it is broken down into tube, bipod, base-plate, and sight for transport.*

CHAPTER 4 Airborne

CHAPTER 4 Airborne

Airborne Infantry

Every time the self-appointed military experts decide that the conventional infantry and especially the parachute infantry is utterly obsolete and will never be used again, some emergency pops up and the 82nd Airborne or the 75th Ranger Regiment's beepers start sounding the recall and the ammunition and grenades start getting issued. These predictions have been made regularly for the past 50 years, especially by advocates of the Air Force, and haven't yet been validated. Soldiers still sing the old cadence count while they run that begins when the sergeant sings the first line, the soldiers sing the response in time to the cadence, the beat being marked by the impact of everybody's left foot, reinforced by each soldier clapping at the same moment. It begins,

"C-One-Thirty, rolling down the strip!
AIR-BORNE! ALL THE WAY!
Airborne Ranger's gonna take a little trip!
AIR-BORNE!
RAAAN-GER!
ALL THE WAY!
Stand up, hook up, shuffle to the door!
AIR-BORNE! ALL THE WAY!
Airborne!
AIR-BORNE!
Ran-ger!
RAN-GER!
All the way!"

RIGHT: *Paratroopers of the 82nd Airborne waddle to their aircraft at Pope Air Force Base, co-located with Fort Bragg, North Carolina. Those rucks look heavy, but they are nothing compared to real-world combat operations when each man will struggle with loads up to 125 pounds. The long cases are weapons containers. Everybody is just as miserable as they appear, and in many cases, worse. Now they will endure a bumpy ride in a C-130 and will anxiously await the command, OUTBOARD PERSONNEL, STAND UP! and the opportunity to get out of the aircraft and out of the harness.*

LEFT: *Staff Sgt. Frank Luedtke is the S-3 Air NCO for 1st Battalion, 319th Airborne Field Artillery, and that serious expression comes from serious responsibilities. He has three UH-60 Black Hawk helicopters inbound, his battery's guns are all prepped for air movement, and his soldiers haven't done this with each other for a very long time. It is his job to make sure everybody is talking to each other, that everybody, as soldiers like to say, is "playing off the same sheet of music."*

PREVIOUS PAGE: *All dressed up with no place to go, students from the Basic Airborne Course wait for the rain to stop and the clouds lift and the opportunity to make their very first jump. They have been JMPIed (Jump Master Personnel Inspection) and are ready to go…to sleep. Until a few years ago, they would be singing the traditional song, BLOOD ON THE RISERS, a ritual familiar to generations of paratroopers, but no longer politically correct.*

Airborne soldiers and Rangers are constantly on standby to draw weapons, ammunition, and all their combat equipment and report to Fort Bragg's legendary Green Ramp where, over and over, they are launched into battle. Despite its complexity, cost and tremendous danger, the insertion of infantry by parachute to seize hostile ground remains one of the fundamental tactics of the U.S. Army.

Paratroopers have a legendary reputation that, for the U.S. Army, goes back to jumps in World War II. But those same modern paratroopers will tell you, as their grandfathers would as well, that the parachute only gives them a ride to the battlefield. Once on the ground, they fight the same kind of battles with the same kind of tactics as employed by conventional (known as "leg," or "God-damned leg") infantry. Well, not exactly like normal infantry—airborne assaults put a very lightweight, very vulnerable force on the ground, without the "tail" that supports conventional ground forces.

The 82nd Airborne, the sole survivor of the old airborne divisions, can put an infantry brigade on the ground almost anywhere in the world at short notice, complete with their artillery, engineering vehicles, some anti-tank systems, and enough batteries, ammunition, water, and MREs for about one day's fighting. If that brigade is fighting a typical enemy force without much armor or artillery, they will quite likely prevail. But all American airborne units are at tremendous risk when facing even lightweight enemy armored vehicles like the BMP or BRDM so common around the globe. Paratroopers don't have time to dig deep holes and don't bring a lot of anti-armor missiles on a jump. They don't even bring a lot of ammunition. They have to depend on the surprise and shock of the prep fires delivered by the Air Force on the area around the drop zone, then the shock and surprise of a few hundred paratroopers dropping in, uninvited. Those paratroopers have to seize their objectives quickly to enable the Air Force to bring in ("air-land" is the term commonly used) follow-on forces and resupply. That's what they've done in Grenada and Panama, and in both places airborne assaults have been successful.

Paratroopers are extreme traditionalists, and one of the traditions is trying to jump with too much gear. This habit started in World War II when the soldiers could barely climb into their C-47s, even with a boost from their buddies, because of all the extra grenades, ammunition, spare sox, and more dubious items required by their commands. The result was that these jumpers were pinned to the DZ when they arrived, or suffered injury while landing, or drowned when making water landings because of overloading.

After a few of these experiences, the 82nd and 101st Airborne Divisions adjusted the loads carried, but these lessons learned were pretty well forgotten when Rangers jumped into Grenada in 1983, and again in Panama in 1989. In both cases, jumpers left the aircraft with rucks weighing up to 120 pounds and even the toughest troopers couldn't move fast or far with loads like those.

Air Assault Infantry

The airborne infantry is the lightest of the light fighting divisions, but certainly not the only one. Fort Campbell, Kentucky, is home base for the legendary 101st Airborne (Air Assault) Division, another of the light fighters. It was a sad day for many old soldiers in 1968 when the 101st was converted from a parachute division to one that rode to the battlefield in helicopters, but the division still conducts the same sort of combat operations in the same sorts of bad neighborhoods, and the division now has a new reputation as good as the old. New Air Assault troopers learn how the division made its night drop into Normandy to secure the D-Day beachhead for the "leg" divisions who waded ashore on 6 June 1944, and how it was the 101st, with nothing much but a tolerance for suffering, that held the key town of Bastogne against the last gasp of Germany's army six months later. It is a fine history of doing much with little, an art form well developed at Campbell.

Air assault operations were pioneered by the old 11th Air Assault Division during the early stages of American involvement in the war in southeast Asia, but American helicopter units were adept at the game well before even that ancient time. We were conducting air assaults in the central highlands in 1962, and even then the techniques were quite routine because my battalion had been doing them for a year. Here's how a typical air assault has been executed by the U.S. Army for the past four decades:

A heli-borne infantry combat assault is used, first of all, to put a lot of agile combat power in important places where the enemy is not likely to be expecting it. A commander might want to use an air assault to raid a suspected enemy base, or headquarters, or supply point. As with parachute assaults, it is a way to put a lot of soldiers right on top of important terrain, like an airfield, a bridge or a mountain pass, where enemy forces could prevent friendly forces from completing their missions.

The whole process begins well in advance with a warning order from the task force commander who will indicate approximately what he wants to do, and who he wants to do it, and when, and why. Once that warning is given, everybody participating in the attack will begin scurrying around, all at once, to prepare. The aviation component of the assault—all the pilots, crews, the maintainers, and their command group, are the bus service that will deliver the infantry from where they get picked up to where they get dropped off. The pick-up point, or PZ, can be a long way from where the helicopters are when the order comes down, and the flight time to collect these soldiers has to be factored in. While one part of the "intel shop" is figuring out how many helicopters will be available and how many troops need to be transported (quickly generating the first of many important statistics, the number of "lifts," or combat sorties

required), other specialists are trying to decide how to get in and back out, where the enemy air defence artillery (ADA) assets are—and which to avoid, and which will have to be suppressed.

At the same time, the ground force is getting its own act together. The ground force commander will already have his order and he now passes it along to his subordinates. The individual soldiers are part of this process, too, and every person will have a lot of preparation to do. For the soldiers who will actually go on the ground, this will be largely familiar because they've rehearsed it all so often. They'll draw their weapons, collect their rucks, NVGs, sign out their personal weapons, draw their ASIP (Advanced SINCGARS System Improvement Program) radios, batteries, ammunition, M18 smoke grenades, M67 fragmentation grenades, M18 Claymore mines, C4 explosive blocks, coils of "det" cord, blasting caps and fuse lighters.

Each squad will be formed up by its leader, a Sergeant E-5, who will conduct a pre-combat personnel inspection. Besides checking each man for ID tags correctly silenced, gas mask, LBE (properly adjusted, complete with first aid pouch and packet), full magazines in pouches, and everything secured with "dummy cord" per unit SOP) squad leaders make sure that each man has recently zeroed his weapon and that the PAC-4 laser illuminator and sight have been aligned

LEFT: *The T-10 parachute is a very slightly improved version of the same system that has been used by American paratroopers for over half a century. This jumper, about one hundred feet above the drop zone, should now assume a good "prepare to land" position – feet and knees together, knees slightly bent, eyes on the horizon, ready to execute a good PLF (parachute landing fall).*

PREVIOUS PAGE: *The ranks of units like the 82nd Airborne are filled with ghosts of soldiers and times and places in the past. Soldiers are encouraged to become historians in many large and small ways. These are the battle streamers of the 82nd, visible at all formal events fluttering from the peak of the staff supporting the American flag. This streamer recalls St. Mère Eglise and the battle for the beach head at the beginning of the Normandy invasion that kicked off on the night of 5–6 June 1944.*

BELOW: *It's not, as the recruiting slogan says, an Army of One, it is really An Army of Us. Nobody in the Army fights alone, but as part of teams of individuals who depend on each other, like this fire team of Airborne infantry soldiers. Groups like this make squads, platoons, companies, battalions, and brigades, and ultimately the Army itself.*

and are secure. Each soldier must show his ID card. If the squad leader is an old combat soldier, he's likely to have each man jump up and down a couple of times to see if anything clanks or rattles. Really old sergeants will sometimes have each man walk a few meters, and sometimes this way he'll find one with an injury or bad boot that results in a limp. Better find out about it now than when the squad is ten klicks from a PZ and has a man who's gone lame.

While the soldiers are getting dressed for the party and putting on their make-up, the Air Force will be assigning aircraft to escort duty and loading rockets and ammunition for their guns. Aircraft and artillery can both prepare (or "prep," as everybody says) the assault landing zone and any threats along the way in or out. The crews of AC-130s, A-10s, and Army AH-64s are the likely candidates for this part of the assault. Their crews will each have their roles, each have their part to play, and the whole thing is organized and choreographed with the precision of a Las Vegas floor show where timing is worked out to the second. All deliberate combat operations involve complex planning on dozens of levels, but air assaults are incredibly intense. Done properly, such an assault puts overwhelming combat power on a critical place at a critical time, with a big payoff.

But when an air assault goes bad, there are few better ways to produce disaster. Helicopters are very vulnerable to ground fire as they approach and depart the LZ—proverbial

RIGHT: *What the well-dressed, super-duper, paratrooper wears to work: T-10 main parachute, reserve, ALICE rucksack, Kevlar helmet, and M16 rifle in weapon container.*

BELOW: *Training never stops, leadership never stops, and any idle moment is a chance for improvement. A M119 gun crew without a fire mission and bored, have an impromptu competition – the ammo cans are full of 105mm fuses, and are heavy. The watch says it's been one minute, forty-five seconds…*

"sitting ducks" full of fuel and soldiers, easily hit with a burst of fire from an AK or RPG. Door gunners can provide suppressive fire during the run in and out, but only at one target at a time. The Army has lost hundreds of helicopters over the years to ground fire, and thousands of brave soldiers and aircrew, too.

One hazard for the initial assault element is the possibility that the enemy will let the first flight land and off-load their soldiers—a company's worth, perhaps—before popping out of the woodwork to engage. Now the enemy is mixed in with the friendlies, probably surrounded, and if the bad guys are any good at all, with mortars dropping in on the concentrated units. The helicopters run the literal and figurative risk of having their tails shot off if they come in to extract the company or even just its rapidly mounting casualties. They will try anyway, and what usually happens is that you've got a few smashed, dead, helicopters burning in the LZ, cluttering up the place and adding to the woes of all concerned. If there is anything that haunts the planning staff of units preparing for air assault operations, it is the battalions of ghosts of American fighting men who've died when the G2 shop misread the ability of the enemy to defend the LZ.

Air Assault School

So the 101st and its merry band of brothers (and a few sisters, too) work diligently to make these things go like clockwork. First is the preparation of the individual soldiers for this special kind of operation. If the 82nd Airborne and the other parachute-delivered units have their school and their wings, so does the air assault community.

The course has three phases, all based on skills and techniques developed and perfected in the old 11th Air Assault Division at Fort Benning in 1964, and in Vietnam afterwards. The first is the Combat Assault portion where soldiers learn how to be safe around helicopters—don't walk into the tail rotor, please, it makes such a mess, and try not to fall out of the open door in flight. Also try not to drop any grenades or inadvertently fire your personal weapon while in the aircraft. These things and more have been tried, with sad results for all concerned. Students also learn the basics of casualty evacuation by helicopter, a skill that will get a workout in the real world of helicopter combat operations. It is a ten-day or two-week program that is an ordeal perhaps more demanding than the current Basic Airborne Course, and concludes with the presentation of wings worthy of at least the same respect.

It begins at 0500 on Day Zero with a quick trip through hell in the form of a demanding obstacle course that challenges each student's strength, courage and resolve. The first obstacle alone sometimes eliminates up to eight or ten percent of the incoming class—climb a rope up about 15 feet, pull yourself up on a grid, step from one beam to the next without falling to the ground, then climb up another 15 feet or so on widely spaced logs, and then climb down a cargo net to the ground. A "no-go" on this one gets you kicked out of the school before you even get started. Eight other obstacles, including the Confidence Climb, Low

OPPOSITE: *This jumper has assumed the correct "prepare to land" position and will return to earth in another second or so. Without combat equipment, this is called a "Hollywood" jump – it is fun but without any tactical purpose, more like sport parachuting than the serious business of being inserted into a combat environment to engage an enemy.*

RIGHT: *M119 Light Cannon go pretty much anywhere the Airborne goes, under a parachute, or helicopter, or behind a vehicle.*

Crawl, and Low Belly Over, the Weaver, the Swing, Stop, and Jump, follow in rapid succession, and, then, while you are still feeling like you have been run over by a truck, a two-mile run. Ten to fifteen percent of soldiers who attend are eliminated by the end of Day Zero, and go back to their units. Welcome to Air Assault School!

Day One and Two are intense training sessions on the skills needed by individual soldiers during air assault operations, with lots of practical experience, then a 50-question written test. Then each student must demonstrate correctly the hand-and-arm signals used to communicate with helicopter crews, with at least seven of ten being done correctly. The students get to board UH-60 Black Hawk helicopters and go through the motions of an air assault. And, since all this has involved a lot of relaxing sitting and standing around, Day Two concludes with a fast six-mile ruck march for time, with anything over 90 minutes being a no-go.

Day Three begins the Sling-Load part of the program and is considered the most difficult. Students learn to rig vehicles, trailers, cannon, and other heavy, bulky gear for transport as external loads under Chinooks and Black Hawks. Here's where the hand-and-arm signals get put to the practical test and where students discover the joys of getting sand-blasted by the rotor wash of the heavy helicopters. When not hooking up to helicopters, the students are busy memorizing the weights and strengths of all the standard rigs used for sling loads, and being tested on this knowledge. For fun, they do more PT, especially "guerilla drills" and ruck runs.

The last phase of Air Assault School trains students to rappel from helicopters, but the training is done on the 34-foot tower. They learn to tie a Swiss seat and to rappel. Rappelling is an acquired taste and not for everyone. You clip yourself into a nylon rope using the Swiss seat and a carabiner—nothing to it, really. It is easy to use the line as a kind of brake, and if you do it right, you can slide gracefully down the rope in a controlled way, all the way to the ground. The trick, though, is in relaxing and leaning back and letting go. Beginners are petrified and hold on to the rope with a death grip. You can't rappel without relaxing, and sometimes it takes a lot of gentle encouragement from the ever-helpful sergeant instructors on the tower to get the novices to take the great leap of faith.

RIGHT: *During the Battle of the Bulge in December 1944, as the Germans threatened to break through allied lines, one 82nd Airborne sergeant is credited with rallying American soldiers from other units fleeing the onslaught with the comment, "I'm the 82nd Airborne, and this is as far as the bastards are going." True or not, that's as far as the bastards went, and today's soldiers haven't forgotten.*

All of them have rappelled in Basic so this isn't usually a problem. They start on the side of the tower that is covered; this is easier and safer than what follows. Then the students rappel from the open side of the tower, off a skid salvaged from a wrecked UH-1 Huey, and this is trickier. You really have to let go this time—lean way back and push off and drop a bit before braking, or you'll smash your face on the skid. The rappel is straight down, with no support for your feet this time. Once you get the hang of braking, you can zoom down, then slow and stop gracefully at ground level. Nothing to it! Once everybody gets through the tower training, you get a shot at doing it from a helicopter, with all its noise and wind for added distraction, first "Hollywood" style without combat equipment, then a "combat" rappel with ruck and weapon.

You'd think all this would be enough, but it isn't; the course ends with a 12-mile fast ruck march with 30-pound ruck in no more than three hours. Survivors pin on the coveted Air Assault wings—but we got ours in 1964, in the 11th Air Assault Division, just for looking cute, and I still have mine. Lucky thing, too—not a one of us who got that first Air Assault Badge back in 1964 would have made it past that first obstacle in today's Air Assault School. But we had attended and graduated from a different kind of program—

we had been shot at, most of us, and some of us had been hit; we had delivered fighting men to hot LZs under fire, and later extracted them—sometimes dead, usually alive; we had seen what bullets do to helicopters, and to helicopter crews; we had seen where puddles of blood can accumulate in the cockpit; some of us had washed the blood away, but not its lingering memory, or the memory of fine, dead men. A lot of us had fired at enemy soldiers, and some of us hit them. We were fat, never did PT, and didn't know many of the hand-and-arm signals used today, but we knew our business pretty well—and maybe we earned our air assault wings after all.

RIGHT: *There are all sorts of ways to be airborne, and SPIE (Special Purpose Insertion and Extraction) rigging is one of them. It is one way to get people in and out of tight spots where no other option is available, and a technique pioneered through many real world operations in Viet Nam.*

BELOW: *Although parachutes are still used to put combat soldiers on the ground from time to time, helicopters offer many advantages for commanders. They can pick things up as well as drop them off, the injury rate is lower, and – best of all – they are organic to the 82nd, unlike the C-17s of the Air Force, and much easier to "lay on."*

The UH-60 Black Hawk is an evolutionary step up from the old UH-1 Huey, now entirely retired. With two powerful gas turbine engines, excellent avionics, and a battle tested airframe and drive train, the Black Hawk has become a reliable system for the Airborne commander and his staff, requiring only a moderate amount of maintenance. It can absorb considerable battle damage, operate in NOE (nap of the earth) low level flight, day or night, while carrying all the tired soldiers you can cram inside.

PREVIOUS PAGE: *One thing a parachute won't help you with, and that is a quick get-away. These soldiers have just executed an artillery raid, swooping into a remote firing position with a howitzer, firing a few carefully aimed rounds, and then hooking up the gun to another aircraft; now the last of the gunners jump back aboard this Black Hawk and will be gone when the enemy's return fire impacts here in another minute or two.*

INSET: *the 82nd's insignia goes back to World War I when it was a conventional infantry unit comprised of men from many parts of the United States and adopted the motto, "All-Americans."*

RIGHT AND INSET: *Paratroopers of the 82nd Airborne waddle to their aircraft at Pope Air Force Base, co-located with Fort Bragg, North Carolina.*

LEFT: *Capt. Keith Pruitt, of Canton, Texas, commander of Company C, 3rd Battalion, 505th Parachute Infantry Regiment, Fort Bragg, N.C., watches flares rise and keeps communication lines up with a squad in the ridgeline adjacent to him. The flares were released because the soldiers were under fire at Objective Hood in Southeastern Afghanistan. (Photo by Sgt. Reeba Critser/28th Public Affairs Detachment.)*

BELOW *Medics from Task Force 1-64 from the 3rd Infantry Division (Mech), Fort Stewart, Ga. evacuate a simulated causality during a combined live fire exercise held approximately 10 miles from the Iraqi border, December 4, 2002. (Photo by Sgt. 1st Class David K. Dismukes.)*

ABOVE RIGHT: *Pfc. Greg Ludmanen, gunner, Company C, 1st Battalion, 325th Airborne Infantry Regiment, lights up the night as paratroopers from the 82nd Airborne Division's 2nd Brigade Combat Team conduct night exercises inside a MOUT city. The light infantry paratroopers are training to prepare for any possible contingency. (Photo by Spc. Brent Williams from Camp Champion, Kuwait of the 49th Public Affairs Detachment (Airborne).)*

RIGHT: *Members of the 82nd Airborne Division, Alpha Company, Ft. Bragg, N.C., fire 60mm mortars on January 16, 2003, in order to illuminate the outer perimeter of Bagram AB, Afghanistan. (U.S. Air Force photo by Staff Sgt. Cherie A. Thurlby.)*

ABOVE: *Operations in Afghanistan were typified by Operation Viper, searching for members of the Taliban and weapons that could be used against forces fighting the war on terrorism in support of Operation Enduring Freedom. Here, Soldiers from Charlie Company 2/504th Parachute Infantry Regiment, Fort Bragg, N.C., walk to their next objective after searching the village of Basleng, 17 February 2003.*

LEFT: *A soldier of B Co. 2nd of the 504th Parachute Infantry Regiment (PIR) White Devils out of Kandahar Army Airfield, Afghanistan watches for enemy forces, while others conduct a searches for suspected Taliban and weapon caches.*

ABOVE: *Another view of the White Devils attached to HHC 1st Brigade 82nd Airborne Division Kandahar Army Airfield, Afghanistan.*

RIGHT: *Soldiers of the 1st of the 504th Parachute Infantry Regiment (PIR) Blue Devils, out of Solerno, Afghanistan conduct a search for suspected Taliban and weapons of a compound in the City of Naray, during Operation Devil Shock on 24 January 2003.*

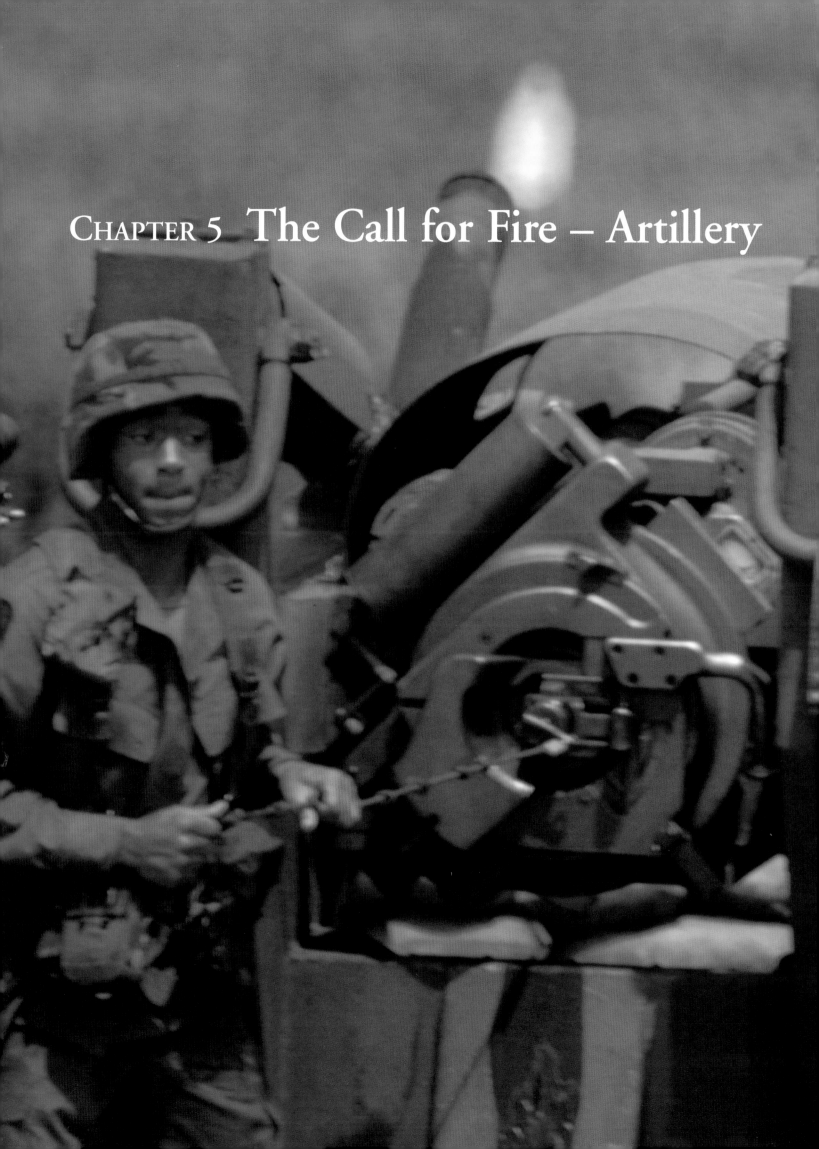

CHAPTER 5   The Call for Fire – Artillery

CHAPTER 5 The Call for Fire – Artillery

Overview

Of all the Army's dark arts, artillery is among the most mysterious. The "redlegs" (as artillerymen are informally called) accurately engage targets so far away that they can't be seen. These targets can be on the far side of a hill or a mountain, tucked into a ravine or obscured by trees. Within moments of "the call for fire," 100-pound steel projectiles filled with high explosive are launched into space on a journey that may last 20 or 30 seconds. These massive shells, when they come back to earth, can flip a main battle tank upside down with a near miss, disassemble it into its components with a direct hit, demolish several or a dozen trucks, or kill entire squads with a single round. One modern M109 artillery battery and its six big self-propelled cannon, when properly supplied with ammunition, can utterly dominate all the battlefield within a 15-mile radius. Battles are not won with artillery alone but without some sort of indirect fire support, they are easily lost.

The array of artillery systems used by the U.S. Army is really quite diverse. The smallest and most portable are the mortars, the last vestige of the smoothbore, muzzle-loading cannon of yore. Infantry companies typically include several 60mm mortar teams to provide immediate, "organic," indirect fire support. Infantry battalions and their weapons

LEFT: *Lt. Col. Williams commands 3rd Battalion, 19th Field Artillery, 4th ID, Fort Hood, Texas.*

PREVIOUS PAGE: *Tube artillery is fired pretty much the same way today as it was 150 years ago, with the same command, and even with a primer and lanyard that closely resemble those used during the American Civil War. The command from the section chief is FIRE, and the Number Two man "pulls the tail" (as "red legs" call the firing lanyard) on the piece to launch one hundred pounds of steel and explosives downrange. This M198 towed cannon is conducting a "direct fire" mission at a visible target only a kilometer or so away, but it can reach much farther than that, striking with precise accuracy 30km and beyond with special ammunition.*

OPPOSITE: *Breech of the M119 Light Gun, a British design modified for American service, in this case with the 82nd Airborne. While most of the rest of the US Army has abandoned the 105mm round as a bit too small for effective reach and target effect, it still makes sense for the light units. With them, its portability by helicopter, for gun, ammunition, and other essentials, can mean the difference between having fire support or doing without.*

BELOW: *When the M109A6 Paladin self propelled howitzer fires, you can actually watch the projectile as it leaves the muzzle and begins its long journey through space. The fireball here (Charge Six Green Bag) is moderate compared to that with a Charge Seven — Red Bag, the most powerful available.*

platoons operate 81mm mortars with longer reach and heavier punch. Some brigades, especially in the mechanized units, have the resources to field 4.2-inch heavy mortars, but these are too heavy to be transported except by vehicle.

Then there are the towed cannon. The Army is currently using just two towed cannon, the M198, a 155mm gun that provides long range fire against enemy assembly areas, troop and vehicle concentrations, convoys, and other high value targets. A British gun, the M119, fires 105mm ammunition; its light weight, innovative trails, and robust design made it a success story in the Falklands, virtues that have endeared it to American light infantry units like the 7th ID, 82nd Airborne, 101st Airborne, and 10th Mountain Divisions. Both these cannon are frequently seen suspended beneath helicopters which deliver them to firing positions in obscure and unlikely parts of the battlefield. They execute a fire mission and then are gone before the enemy can fire back, a tactic called an artillery raid.

Heavier divisions, especially the armored ones, rely upon

LEFT: *Prepared 155mm projectiles, ready to load and fire. The fuse is a PD, or "point-detonating," type that will initiate the powder train that will ultimately cause the TNT to explode.*

OPPOSITE, ABOVE: *Missile out! A TOW missile is dispatched from an armored scout humvee. The gunner acquires his target in the sight, centers the crosshairs on the victim, and presses two switches on the right hand grip. One switch energizes the system, the other fires it. Both must be depressed during the entire time of flight, about ten seconds by the clock but an eternity in combat. There is a slight delay after the gunner presses the trigger, about a second and a half, before a gas generator fires and pops the missile out of the tube. Only after it is about ten meters downrange will the rocket motors fire, pushing the TOW along, not in a straight line but in a series of jerky little bobs and weaves. The gunner must ignore all these distractions and keep the button down and the sight picture centered till impact, just one of the essential skills of today's combat soldier.*

OPPOSITE, BELOW LEFT: *Artillery batteries have a huge appetite for ammunition and the unsung heroes of the business of putting steel on target are the soldiers who keep the guns fed. These are standard HE (high explosive) projectiles, the big bullets that are launched downrange. Each weighs about 100 pounds and is a special steel container filled with TNT explosive. The eye on top of each is a shipping plug and is removed when the round is prepared for firing.*

LEFT: *Fort Sill is the home of American artillery, for both the US Army and Marine Corps, where "red legs" have learned their dark art for many generations. This ceremonial reenactment of the old horse-drawn artillery of nearly a hundred years ago rehearses on the polo field where parades and reviews have been held since territorial days and the Indian Wars.*

the M109 Paladin self-propelled howitzer. This system, whose foundation is now 40 years old, specializes in supporting armored attacks, cleaning out enemy artillery batteries that would otherwise threaten tanks and AFVs.

And for the deepest fire missions, heavy units normally deploy the Multiple Launch Rocket System, or MLRS. Each of these tracked vehicles typically fires six free-flight rockets. Each rocket carries a warhead stuffed with small sub-munitions that scatter over a target and detonate on contact with the ground or anything on it. Together, they sanitize an area about the size of a football field, killing personnel and destroying tanks, trucks, radar vans, missile launchers, or enemy tactical operations centers.

M119

As mentioned above, the 105mm M119 Light Gun is a battle-tested design. It is light, with a lot of aluminum alloy components, intended for air-mobile operations, especially artillery raids. Although the 105mm round is becoming a bit too small for general use on the modern battlefield, where the 155mm projectile is standard in almost every army, light units can't afford either the "tooth" or the "tail" of the M198 or M109 cannon. If the 82nd or 101st want reliable, organic, artillery support, they're going to hope for close air support from the Air Force or from Corps, but they will normally depend on their own guns, the M119s.

One of the M119's many virtues is that it can go into action within a very few minutes from the moment a Black Hawk helicopter or a HMMWV (or Humvee, the Army's modern version of the Jeep of World War II fame) drops it off at a firing point. Since the same aircraft or vehicle can

LEFT: *Not quite sunrise and these gunners are already saluting the dawn with one of the first M119 105mm cannons built by Royal Ordnance for the US Army. The M119 is a very light, agile gun for its type, features that made it a hit with British forces during the Falklands campaign. There, Puma helicopters moved gun, ammunition, and gunners into remote firing positions where they surprised Argentine enemies with effective artillery fire when none was anticipated.*

INSET, LEFT: *An M119 rigged for movement as a helicopter external load. Artillery units must be proficient in all sorts of skills besides the theory and practice of accurate gunnery, and learning how to rig cannon for helicopter "gun raids" and put them into action are part of the program for novice "thirteen-bravos," the military occupational specialty for "cannon crewmembers."*

INSET, RIGHT: *Two projectiles prepared for firing. American tube artillery uses "semi-fixed" ammunition – the projectile and propellant case are only brought together just before firing. This permits a wide range of customized charges and projectiles and fuses to be mixed and matched as ordered by the FDC (fire direction center) where the missions are plotted.*

carry the crew and a small supply of ammunition at the same time, fire missions can be executed almost immediately. The crew of seven or eight (typically, less if necessary) can be "good to go" in about three minutes, first dropping the circular firing platform, then installing the sight and orienting the tube to an azimuth sent by radio from the FDC (Fire Direction Center).

The M119 uses the same "semi-fixed" kind of ammunition that has been standard for many years. Crews get the rounds in individual fiberboard tubes nearly identical to those used by their grandfathers in World War II, and the contents look nearly identical, too. Inside are a metallic case and projectile. The case contains a primer and the propellant, with the "powder" (which is really the size and shape of macaroni) in several numbered bags. The projectile does not have a fuse installed—that is shipped separately for safety reasons.

When the FDC calls down for a status check, the sergeants who are "chief of section" (COS) radio back, "Gun One, ready," "Gun Two, ready," until they are all good to go. A selection of ammunition will by now have been taken out of the shipping tubes, with fuses installed in the projectiles but unset. The gun crew stand by while the FDC crew gets itself "unscrewed", a process that can take seconds or hours. Finally, the radio operator at each gun gets the call "Fire mission." He repeats, "FIRE MISSION," and every member of the crew repeats the warning order, scurrying to his assigned position.

On command, the propellant charge is "cut"—the FDC will specify the number of propellant increments to be used, up to seven for maximum velocity and potential range with

LEFT: *The 155mm projectile leaves the muzzle at under 900 meters per second, slow enough to photograph easily. Paladin have an automatic fire control system that permits the crew to fire within a minute or so of reaching a firing position, then taking off again before counter-battery fire can be returned.*

OPPOSITE, ABOVE: *This PD, or point-detonating fuse is only installed in the fuse well of the projectile when the gun is in position and nearly ready to conduct fire missions. It has two possible settings, "super quick" and "delay." The normal setting is SQ and results in jagged steel shards, often looking like rough saws, being sprayed across an wide area, very effective against troops in the open, refueling points, command and control points, and similar targets. When set to Delay, however, the shell will penetrate into the dirt before detonation, a feature that makes it more effective against bunkers or prepared positions.*

OPPOSITE, BELOW: *The M109 has been around for a long time and will probably be in the inventory for another twenty years, perhaps longer. Although the basic hull and turret haven't changed a lot since the 1950s, the cannon and fire control systems are entirely new in the current A6 variant, the Paladin, like these from the 4th Infantry Division, almost ready to move into their firing positions.*

conventional HE rounds. That's 11.5km, and 14km for Charge Eight; using the M913 RAP (rocket-assisted projectile) the M119 can shoot at targets 19km away. In emergencies, it can put out six rounds a minute, but only for two minutes. Sustained firing missions with the light gun can launch three rounds per minute for 30 minutes—if the supply system can keep up.

M109

Fire missions happen quickly, with all members of the gun crew performing their individual responsibilities with the coordinated precision of a championship football team. It begins, on the A6 version of the M109, with a display appearing on the Automatic Fire Control system panel in front of the section chief. He shouts "Fire mission!" – his warning order to the crew. They all acknowledge by replying, "Fire mission," and go to their positions.

The driver, who will be sitting in his seat in the left forward part of the hull, revs the engine, which has been idling, up to provide hydraulic pressure to operate the gun-laying systems. Firing data appears on the AFS and the section chief calls it out – fuse type, projectile type, propellant charge, deflection, and quadrant. "HE," he orders, "PD, Charge 4 Green Bag, deflection thirty-two hundred, quadrant four hundred!" The gunner and Number One man

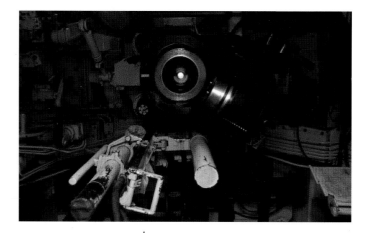

OPPOSITE: *Not much holds the hundred-pound projectile on the tray, just small steel lips that engage the rear of the copper driving bands. Although it doesn't happen often, occasionally a projectile will slip off and fall to the deck. The primary danger is having it land on your foot, not having the thing explode, since the fuse is designed to operate only after the shell is fired.*

RIGHT, FROM TOP TO BOTTOM:
Breech of the M284 cannon installed on the Paladin.

Each cannon is under the control of a sergeant, the Chief of Section, who receives and executes fire missions sent from the FDC. On the A6 Paladin, this process is much more automated than on earlier models. The screen on the bulkhead in front of this sergeant is his AFS, or automatic fire control system, and it displays missions and will actually lay the gun on the target.

155mm HE projectile on the loading tray. Only after receiving a fire mission, and only after the section chief verifies the proper projectile is on the tray, will the power rammer (visible to the left of the projectile) be used to load and ram the shell.

Another link with the past, propellant still is supplied in linen bags just as in the ancient days of muzzle-loading cannon during the 19th Century. This system allows propellant charges to be "cut," or customized, for different ranges.

watch the screen, verifying the data. Number One pulls a projectile from the rack, with a PD – "point-detonating" – fuse already screwed into the fuse well. Although the projectile weighs just under 100 pounds, he moves it quickly and easily to the loading tray.

"Shell HE, ready to be verified!" Number One reports. The section chief looks at the projectile on the tray, confirms the fuse type and shell type, then confirms that it is ready to be rammed by calling, 'Verified!"

"Permission to ram?" asks Number One.

"Ram!"

Number One operates the switch that actives the power rammer; the heavy projectile is pushed forward, off the tray and seated in the chamber. The loading tray now swings down and out of the way. In the very few seconds required for this to occur, the gunner has been cutting the propellant charge. From a steel canister, also at the rear of the turret, the gunner has extracted a set of propellant bags tied together with long fabric strips. Deftly, from long practice, the gunner unties the bundle, removes the top propellant bag, clearly labeled with a 5, and sets it aside. Now he quickly ties the charge back up with the strips and presents it to the section chief for inspection.

"Charge Four, Green Bag, ready to be verified," the gunner says to the section chief.

LEFT: *Primers are installed in the breech only after the other components are loaded and the gun nearly ready to fire. They closely resemble common rifle cartridge cases, and fulfill the same function, igniting the propellant and sealing the chamber.*

ABOVE RIGHT: *Automatic Fire Control display. This screen actually can be used many ways and is part of the US Army's program to incorporate secure digital communications across the battlefield, generically known as Force XXI Battle Command, Brigade and Below, but invariably called "F B C B Two."*

RIGHT: *It is quite possible for the Paladin and older M109s to engage in direct fire missions against visible targets, although that doesn't happen often. The control in the center of the photo, identical in function to the gun control on a tank, is used to provide direct control of the tube's orientation and elevation.*

NEXT PAGE: *Not far from the firing batteries will be found the ammunition re-supply points and their huge, rough terrain trucks and forklifts. A tremendous amount of manpower is required to unpack the palletized projectiles, propellant tubes, and fuse boxes, and despite the crane to assist with the process, each component is currently hand-carried to the FASV, the Field Artillery Supply Vehicle, each of which carries sixty rounds and accompanies one M109.*

The section chief visually inspects the charge, confirms that it is color-coded green, sees bags one, two, three, and that the last bag is labeled 4. He says "Verified." The gunner turns toward the breech, inserts the charge, then reports, "I see red to the rear!" This confirms that the igniter pad, full of old-style black powder used to ignite the rest of the charge, will face the primer. Then he reports, "Closing the breech!" The huge breechblock slams shut, sealing the chamber. The gunner insures that the breech is fully closed by inspecting two white marks, one on the breechblock, the other on the breech itself – they must align.

Now the section chief lays the gun on the target. With older guns, this used to involve a lot of cranking and careful alignment of the optical sight. The M109A6's automatic fire control system lays the gun to the data provided by the battery, simply by pressing the LAY key on the AFS screen. The section chief holds the key down and the computer goes to work. Hydraulic pressure swings the gun and elevates it with speed and precision, and when the tube is aligned, the LAY indicator lights up.

"The LAY light is lit," calls the section chief. "Deflection and quadrant match! No warning messages!" The gunner looks at the AFS screen over the section chief's shoulder, and then he confirms that the gun is ready to fire by reporting, "Verified!"

Despite all this modern computer technology, the gun is fired with a lanyard exactly like that used by gunners 150 years ago, almost exactly the same way, and exactly on the same command. A primer, resembling a common rifle cartridge case, is inserted in a chamber at the rear of the breechblock, and the gun is nearly ready to fire. The AFS display shows FIRE WHEN READY. Till now, the section chief has held onto the short length of rope with a steel hook on the end, the firing lanyard. Now he hands it to the Number One many with the command, "Hook up." The gunner engages the hook into the hammer, takes up the slack in the lanyard, and looks at the section chief, awaiting his order. That order is made with both a gesture and voice command – the section chief points to the gunner at the same time he orders, "FIRE!" Even with Charge Four, the gun recoils heavily and the whole vehicle rocks backward. The breechblock drops as the gun recovers and the turret interior fills with spent propellant gasses until a blower exhausts them. Number One drops the lanyard and picks up a swab, inserts it into the chamber, quickly cleaning any residue, then as the smoke clears, he inspects the bore to make sure the projectile made it all the way out. "Bore clear," he reports.

"End of mission," the Fire Direction Center calls on the radio, and the crew relaxes until it is time to do it all over again. From start to finish, the whole process has taken only about fifteen seconds.

Have Gun, Will Travel
(Older Americans will remember a TV show about a gunfighter named Paladin; the show always opened with his business card that read "have gun, will travel" and is surely the original source for the name of this system.. Army artillery brigade commanders have been relying on the M109 Paladin for generations. It is a successful system, another design that goes all the way back to the Korean War, and one that is in use around the world by many nations. These same commanders were hoping desperately that the Crusader, an advanced mobile gun system with autoloader and all the other advanced technologies, would soon replace the M109, but the cost of the new system killed it. The old Paladin is going to keep on shooting instead of being retired, although most of them are pretty well worn out.

M109s are easily confused with tanks by civilians, but under the skin the differences are enormous. They are tracked vehicles about the same size as an Abrams M1A2, with a turret and large gun, but are a bit bulkier overall. And while they may look heavily armored, the appearance is deceiving; anything heavier than a .50-caliber round or small artillery shell fragment can penetrate the Paladin's fairly thin hide. And the gun, while about the size of a tank's cannon, fires a different kind of projectile in a very different kind of way.

The junior man on the crew, often a PV2 or PFC, will normally be the driver—it's where you get acquainted with the beast and with the business of heavy artillery without too much risk of killing the wrong people. He drives from the front left, in his own little compartment. He also does exactly what he is told and helps out with all the chores around the vehicle. It is his primary responsibility to make sure it is fueled, oiled, and ready to go when the section chief calls, "Driver, move out!"

Inside the turret, any tanker will marvel at all the room—and the large, uncluttered deck, and any tanker will be thinking, "What a great place to sleep out of the rain!" At the rear of the turret are rows of racks and bins each holding a fused projectile or propellant canister. More racks hold additional projectiles tucked into odd places around the hull—high-explosive, illumination, and smoke being the most common types, but with many others available. Among the more exotic of these are the very expensive, very precise Copperhead laser-guided projectiles normally used for first-round hits on high priority targets.

The M109's gun uses separate-loading ammunition, just like the M198 towed howitzer. The projectile alone weighs about 100 pounds, and is loaded first, rammed mechanically, then the propellant bags are inserted in the breech, the breech block is closed, and a primer inserted. The Challenger and other really modern SP guns now use auto-loaders, but not Paladin.

ABOVE: *Field artillery observers are one of several critical links to "putting steel on target." While most "FOs" today have digital message devices and precision viewing systems with laser rangefinders, the whole process still depends on trained and experienced soldiers and the "Mk One Eyeball."*

RIGHT: *Fire missions are now designed largely by computer systems linked to the firing batteries by secure digital communications, and instead of plotting boards and slide rules, members of the Fire Direction Center (FDC) use computers to produce data for the guns. They are still working out of an old M113, however, just as FDCs have been doing for forty years.*

RIGHT: *Indirect fire artillery couldn't hit anything without its eyes and ears, the forward observers who spot the threats, call them in, correct impacts, the whole time being closer to the enemy than anybody else. This job requires excellent fieldcraft skills – the ability to use cover and concealment, to live extended periods under very austere conditions, and move from one position to another on foot if necessary. Devices like this new LRASSS (Long Range Advanced Scout Surveillance System) can identify and designate targets at 20km ranges, through dust, fog, and dark of night…at a cost of about half a million dollars a copy.*

OPPOSITE, ABOVE: *Specialist Thompson is a member of a 4th Infantry Division scout platoon and uses the traditional map, compass, and Mk One Eyeball, along with common sense and advanced technology, to support the maneuver commander.*

OPPOSITE, BELOW: *Scouts use all sorts of imaging devices, including this compact, lightweight one for closer targets. A laser rangefinder provides distance information but, unlike the larger systems, isn't used for designating precision munitions/*

LEFT: *Even MLRS rocket launchers sometimes fire blanks. This rocket lacks a warhead because it is part of a test and evaluation program for an improved motor assembly.*

INSETS: *Even just one man can execute fire missions with the MLRS, although it goes faster with the usual three. Once in position, the launcher is erected and oriented by computer control, then fired from within the cab after the armored shutters are closed.*

CHAPTER 6 Special Operations Forces

Chapter 6 Special Operations Forces

Once the bad boy and unloved stepchild of the Army, the unconventional units are currently America's most successful secret weapon. Most civilians think of this part of the Army, when they think of it at all, as the legendary "Green Berets," but it is a much bigger story than that, and getting bigger all the time. Today's Army Special Operations Forces include the 75th Ranger Regiment (three battalions and a headquarters), seven Special Forces "groups" (each roughly equivalent to a brigade), Delta Force, the 160th Special Operations Aviation Regiment (the "Night Stalkers"), three Psychological Operations Groups (one active duty, two Reserve), and the

96th Civil Affairs Battalion. In addition, all these units are supported by their own dedicated, specially qualified, Signal and Support battalions for communication and supply.

Very Unconventional Warriors—the "Green Berets"
Although virtually all Americans have heard of the "Green Berets," very few know who they are or what they do—or even their proper name, Special Forces. That's just fine with most of these soldiers, too, because they are a pretty shy bunch who typically prefer to deal only with their own community. Years of fictions like the Rambo movies and similar nonsense, along with genuine security concerns, have

PREVIOUS PAGE: *It is a bit early for insertion, but this team is dropping in unexpectedly anyway, with rucks deployed on their lowering lines. Special Forces units conduct a wide variety of missions in many nations around the globe, and they are prepared to get where they need to be using any means necessary.*

LEFT: *Two old soldiers – sergeants Rick Cardin and "Buck" Ravenscroft – wait somewhat patiently while the crew of the aircraft scheduled to deliver them to the drop zone get themselves unscrewed.*

FAR LEFT: *The heritage of modern Special Forces goes back to World War II and the Office of Strategic Services (OSS). Small teams, typically just three people, parachuted into enemy held territory and help organize, equip, and lead irregular forces in occupied France, Italy, Burma, and elsewhere. The motto of SF is a reminder of that heritage – a Latin phrase meaning, "to free the oppressed."*

BELOW LEFT: *Out in the weeds behind battalion headquarters, a couple of commo men – MOS 18E or "Eighteen Echos" – put in a call to a another unit a thousand miles away.*

helped turn the SF community into a very secluded place. But here's the real story on some of the finest, and most interesting, soldiers in the Army.

The traditional first mission of the Special Forces groups is actually more like diplomacy and education than mayhem. SF soldiers are the Army's multi-lingual, multi-cultural evangelists. They go to strange places and help oppressed peoples defend themselves. This involves getting the trust of these people, organizing them, teaching them the fundamentals of military operations, helping them get equipped and armed, and sometimes leading them on operations. This missionary work is called Unconventional Warfare (UW), and I have seen it work wonders in the most unlikely places. It takes a very special soldier to gain the trust of an Afghan warrior, to speak to him in his own tribal dialect, to soldier with him under austere conditions, but that's what SF soldiers have been doing for more than 40 years.

Besides the UW mission, SF teams conduct "Foreign Internal Defense" (FID) training, "Direct Action" (DA) strike missions against enemy targets, and Special Reconnaissance (SR) assignments. Direct action missions are a lot like Ranger assignments—killing people, blowing things up—but an SF detachment will get the call when a more covert infiltration is required, or you have to speak to somebody in Farsi or Urdu before you shoot them.

SF soldiers operate in building block units of 12 men, previously called an A Team, now christened an Operational Detachment Alpha or ODA. Each ODA is theoretically designed to recruit, train, equip, and lead a battalion of indigenous fighters, up to around 500 men. The team structure has two of each critical skill—two administrators, the commander and the warrant officer, two demo men, two commo guys, two engineers, and two medics. When the team operates as a single unit, they back each other up, with cover for when casualties occur. But the team can be split into two half-detachments, too, and operate in different regions at the same time.

The ODAs do the recruiting, patrolling, the strikes and recons, but not without help. Behind each ODA is a B-team, functioning like an Army company's headquarters unit. And behind the ODAs and ODBs, is the C-detachment, the command and control group that keeps the teams supplied out in the weeds, that gathers and presents intel on potential targets, that gets people paid, and that is responsible for the conduct of the missions. These ODCs set up the Forward Operating Bases and function like a battalion headquarters.

Green Berets are amazing people, but seldom in the ways Americans believe. Classic SF missions give sergeants and junior officers tasks that demand a very different kind of courage than what you see in an old Rambo movie. What makes these soldiers remarkable is that they can drop into the most alien of places and make friends, then make soldiers, then conduct effective military missions. That's what they did in Vietnam, and that's what they did in Afghanistan. Who else in the Army today would ride a horse into battle? Who else is required to speak a foreign language, or appreciate a foreign culture?

Within the formal descriptions of SF missions, if you know how to read between the lines, is a requirement for men who have the communication skills, charm, and loyalty of a diplomat—inside the uniform of a staff sergeant or sergeant first class. NCOs who would be far down the food chain in any conventional unit are sometimes effectively responsible for very important relationships with foreign

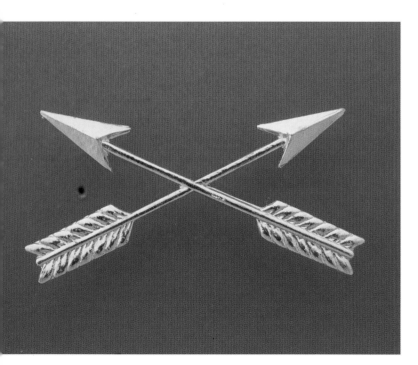

governments. These guys sometimes operate far from any kind of support, in very dangerous locations, and have done so generally with a sense of humor and very effectively. The successful conduct of operations in Afghanistan—which the critics predicted would be an American blood-bath—is a case in point. Green Berets are good at killing people when they have to, but they are unique among American combat organizations that they are just as good at completing missions without shedding any blood at all.

75th Ranger Regiment

In some ways the Ranger Regiment is the antithesis of the Green Berets. Rangers don't need to learn foreign languages or to appreciate foreign cultures, they just want to know where the drop zone is and what they're supposed to destroy. Rangers are (despite what anybody else tries to tell you) the Army's best little assault force, experts at raids, parachute assaults, and inflicting maximum violence in minimum

LEFT: *Members of an A detachment plot and scheme in the traditional way, with a hasty map drawn in the dirt.*

FAR LEFT: *Branch insignia for Special Forces.*

airfield at Point Salines, rescued American medical students, and then used helicopters to finish cleaning out pockets of resisting Cubans and Grenada defense forces.

All three battalions led the assault against Panamanian forces during Operation Just Cause in late December 1989, jumping in to the international airport and a military airfield at Rio Hato. The Regiment lost five men killed and 42 wounded in the operation but captured over a thousand enemy soldiers and 18,000 small arms and crew-served weapons. Six Rangers died during a daylight raid in Mogadishu, Somalia, in 1993 in vicious combat that resulted in about 300 enemy KIA.

One battalion of the Regiment is always ready for combat deployments on extremely short notice, the Ranger Ready Force. By itself or with additional units, a Ranger force is normally tasked with forcing entry for a larger assault force, conducting fierce light infantry combat operations for a short time, then stepping aside for heavier units with heavier firepower.

You can generally spot a Ranger from about 300 meters; nobody stands up straighter, and most of them look like weight lifters. They prefer wearing a patrol cap, normally a sun-bleached and well-worn version, and with a Ranger tab sewn above the rank insignia. And, finally, Rangers tuck the top of their caps in a distinctive way called the Ranger Roll. Their LBE is always well-tricked-out, with everything neatly secured with "dummy cord," with two compasses (one for backup) tucked into a pouch on the belt, a strobe (a rescue beacon, normally used to reveal the position of soldiers on the ground to aircraft overhead), pace counter and snap link on the suspenders. Ranger companies all include specialist teams of highly qualified soldiers—snipers, demolition experts, scout swimmers, HALO and HAHO jumpers (HAHO: high altitude/low opening; HAHO high altitude/high opening—special purpose parachute techniques).

Delta

The Army really doesn't talk about Delta, and maybe we shouldn't, either. Oh, maybe a few little secrets won't hurt. Delta was invented by Colonel Charlie Beckwith and was partly based on the British Army's Special Air Service or SAS. Both are composed entirely of guys and gals closely related to Superman, the strongest of the strong, bravest of the brave.

time. Besides the combat assignment, Rangers are the standard-bearers of the Army, setting a target of personal excellence for soldiers in all MOSs. The motto of the Rangers is "Rangers Lead the Way," and that applies in combat as well as in the routine of garrison. They are recruited from throughout the Army, not just the infantry or combat arms, and are expected to disseminate Ranger values to all kinds of units.

The modern Ranger Regiment has only been part of the Army since 1974 although the tradition is older than the nation—the epitome of light infantry, able to strike effectively in unexpected places, in unexpected ways. Today's Ranger organization prepared to participate in the Iranian hostage rescue in 1980 but didn't launch into battle for another three years, in the 1983 invasion of Grenada, Operation Urgent Fury. On October 25th, 1983, the 1st and 2nd Brigades jumped from 500 feet (combat minimum altitude, too low for using reserve parachutes) to seize the

ABOVE: *Russ Mann, on the left, is First Sergeant for the headquarters company, 3rd Battalion, 12th Special Forces Group (Airborne), and Gerry Schumacher, on the right, is the battalion commander. Both have extensive combat experience and many years in SF.*

ABOVE RIGHT: *The Medal of Honor is America's highest military tribute. It is never "won," but has been awarded 3,428 times to 3,409 recipients since 1863. There are three variations on the Medal of Honor, and this is the one presented to members of the US Army.*

Their missions are similar, to be prepared to execute extremely high-risk covert combat operations—hostage rescues, counter-terrorist strikes, the sorts of missions even Rambo isn't good enough to accomplish. While you'll often see Navy SEALs proclaim who they are with ball caps and decals on their cars, Delta troopers are utterly silent about who they work for and are serious about security in a way not found elsewhere outside the "black ops" community.

It is common knowledge that Delta uses the standard Army "triangular" organization of a headquarters plus three units, called "squadrons," each subdivided into "troops." They train in complete privacy at secluded facilities and behind berms and walls, safe from prying eyes. Those skills have been put to work in Somalia, Panama, Iraq during the Gulf War, and …well, let's just say, other places and other times. Delta recruits from across the whole Army twice each year, looking for people with the right combination of personality, specialized skills, courage, and

aptitude for covert ops. And, while women may be prohibited from the infantry, armor, artillery, or combat engineers, the best of them are welcome here, as long as they can meet the incredibly high standards demanded of the men—and some do, and are recruited. And that is probably all you need to know about Delta, and maybe more.

160th Special Operations Aviation Regiment—"Night Stalkers"

During the war in Southeast Asia, it became painfully apparent that valor wasn't quite enough when it came to providing the kind of aviation support needed by all the "across-the-fence" clandestine operations teams, the "Hatchet Forces," and all the other oddball little units conducting strange missions in strange ways. Helicopter crews and aircraft were trained and equipped for these missions and became especially adept at inserting and extracting teams under fire.

Today's SOF aviators belong to the 160th SOAR, a provisional unit that was "stood up" officially in October 1981 as an experimental task force (called Task Force 160) and has since participated in many hazardous combat operations, public and private. Known as the Night Stalkers for their habit of operating primarily at night, the 160th SOAR got its baptism of fire during Operation Urgent Fury and the invasion of Grenada. The unit helped kick off Operation Just Cause with night air assault operations against Panamanian targets.

Based on this success, TF 160 was expanded in 1990 to regimental size and shape.

160th SOAR operates special upgraded versions of the Chinook, Black Hawk, and Little Bird helicopters, the MH-47, MH-60, and MH-6. The MH-47E is equipped with an in-flight refueling probe, terrain-mapping and -following radar, weather radar, extra fuel capacity, and blades that fold for expedited transport on cargo aircraft or naval vessels. Pilots have a HUD (head-up display), similar to those found in fighter aircraft; this display permits the pilot to keep his or her eyes out of the cockpit and still monitor the aircraft's primary instruments. MH-47Es have dual antennae for satellite radio communications, flat-panel monitors for the crew, and sensors to warn when the aircraft is being engaged by enemy fire-control radar or missiles. MH-47Es can carry 25 Rangers or other SOF soldiers through rain and snow and darkness, at high speed, low altitude, and long distances. An SOF version of the Chinook Delta is equipped with the All Weather Cockpit (AWC). Chinooks have a 20,000ft ceiling making them handy for places like Afghanistan. They don't do as well under such adverse "density altitude" conditions, but they will still get people in and out of tight spots on mountain tops.

At the other end of the helicopter spectrum, Night Stalkers operate the beloved MH-6 Little Bird, a small, agile, quiet, and powerful aircraft based on the old Hughes 500 series. In its early, Vietnam era, configuration, the Little Bird was quite successful at sneaking people in and out of dangerous neighborhoods and also served as a low-level recon aircraft in a way that fixed wing aircraft couldn't equal. It is a delightful helicopter to fly, with incredible visibility for the two pilots, fast, and stable. Although small, it can carry six combat-equipped soldiers into battle—the hard way, because they won't all fit inside. Instead, they stand on the skids outside, or sit on fold-down benches on the latest models. These soldiers can fast-rope down or just jump if they are not too high off the ground. Getting them back out again is a little more difficult, but MH-6s can be equipped with lightweight ladders originally designed for use in cave exploration or mountaineering, made of thin cable and aluminum tube, up which any mission survivors can climb and be hoisted to safety.

MH-60 variants of the Black Hawk include the K and two variants on the L models. All are based on the basic UH-60 airframe but with an in-flight refueling probe and better navigation and survivability systems. The K is tricked out to insert and extract small SOF teams into very hazardous and remote LZs, under extreme weather conditions and, of course, in the dead of night. The L is configured as a big gunfighter, the Direct Action Penetrator (DAP), a kind of giant descendant of the old Huey gunship but carrying far more firepower in the form of guns, rockets, and missiles. MH-60s will normally cruise at 120 knots, dash up to 178 knots, have a maximum range of 450nm and endurance of about 4 hours, 20 minutes.

CHAPTER 7 Army Aviation

Chapter 7 Army Aviation

Aviation has been a part of the Army since the Wright brothers first launched a successful powered heavier-than-air craft a century ago, in 1903. In fact, the first person ever killed in an airplane crash was probably a U.S. Army officer, Lt. Thomas E. Selfridge, in 1908, beginning an Army tradition. Combat aviation is a dangerous business with a big payoff.

Helicopters started becoming important to the Army in the late 1950s when their ability to leapfrog soldiers and their equipment over rough terrain and into roadless areas started to become a practical reality. H-21s and H-34s went to Vietnam in 1961; despite being underpowered, they

proved the concept and wrote the first chapter of the book on airmobility.

Today, the Army has three basic kinds of jobs for its "Airedales" and "rotorheads." One is the "attack" role performed by AH-64 Apaches and involves delivering fire on enemy targets. Another mission, also sometimes accomplished by the Apache in its Longbow variant, involves stealthy reconnaissance—peeping over a ridge or treeline to see what's on the other side. This aerial recon mission is also ably performed by the OH-58, a military version of the Bell Ranger helicopter, and the Delta model of this aircraft, equipped with its "million-dollar beachball" antenna is especially stealthy. This sensor array is mounted on top of the

LEFT: *Chief Warrant Officer John Cooney is an old soldier who has seen some combat. Soldiers with combat experience are authorized to wear the unit insignia of their old unit on the right shoulder – in this case, the legendary 1st Air Cav and Viet Nam.*

FAR LEFT: *Cyclic control, UH-60 Black Hawk. Use of all those buttons, switches, and controls becomes automatic for helicopter pilots, and they are on the grip because it takes two hands to fly a helicopter. The cyclic controls the tilt of the rotor disk, and therefore the direction of movement – including backwards, if desired.*

BELOW LEFT: *A warrant officer pilot and enlisted observer slip the surly bonds of earth for a training mission in an OH-58D scout helicopter. The "Delta" is a major upgrade of the old 58, and that sphere above the rotor head is the "million-dollar-beachball."*

PREVIOUS PAGE: *A pair of AH-64 Apaches prepare to engage targets. Unlike fixed wing aircraft, the pilot is seated in the rear, the weapons officer forward. Both co-pilot/gunners have their heads down, tracking targets and preparing to fire.*

PREVIOUS PAGE, INSET: *The branch insignia for Army aviation officers is identical to that of the old Army Air Corps of World War II, a reminder of an ancient and honorable tradition that goes back to the Wright Brothers.*

BELOW: *Unlike their Air Force brethren, Army aviators are field soldiers and see combat at close range. Major Dwyer is an Apache pilot.*

rotor mast but doesn't rotate with the blades. An OH-58D pilot and his enlisted observer need only expose the ball from behind cover—and anything will do, including buildings—to get a bird's-eye view of the battlefield without being seen in return. And finally there is the airborne express mission, delivering people, weapons, supplies, equipment, fuel, and anything else (within limits) wherever it is needed. This mission is normally executed by UH-60 Black Hawks and CH-47 Chinooks.

LEFT: *Becoming proficient as a helicopter pilot requires many months of intense training and begins for Army aviators at Fort Rucker, Alabama, where pilots and crewmembers have learned their professions for many years.*

BELOW LEFT: *Army helicopter pilots routinely fly NOE or "nap of the earth" missions, with their landing gear skimming the treetops, at high speed, in the middle of the night. Such missions wouldn't be possible without the use of night vision goggles (NVG) like those in this photograph.*

FAR LEFT: *Rangers depend on the Army's own little air force to get them where they need to go, and back out again when it is time to go home. That chore is normally assigned to the 160th Special Operations Air Regiment, a unit trained and equipped for executing the blackest of missions on the darkest of nights.*

AH-64 Apache

The Apache can destroy tanks with its laser-guided Hellfire missiles, or make a mess of a convoy of trucks or an enemy troop concentration with unguided 70mm free-flight rockets, or destroy a single vehicle, bunker, radar antenna, or similar target with cannon fire from its 30mm Chain Gun. It is as agile as any ground-attack fixed-wing fighter, if not quite as fast and the Hellfire missiles are effective to 8km. Apaches can cruise at 145 knots, with a combat endurance of up to three hours when lightly loaded. With internal fuel only, the AH-64 is good for about 150km range, but when the option of up to four 230-gallon auxiliary fuel tanks is used, that range goes up to a lot farther than the crew will want to fly.

Configured for its tank-busting role, Apaches can be tricked out one of several ways. When speed is a priority, ground crews load eight Hellfire missiles, four on pylons attached to each stubby little wing, and 320 rounds of 30mm ammunition for the Chain Gun. Thus lightly loaded, the AH-64 can climb at nearly 1,500 feet per minute. If the commander expects a lot of tanks, the racks can be filled with 16 of the missiles,w but when assigned a covering mission where anything can pop up, two pods with 19 folding-fin 70mm aerial rockets are added to the wings and a lot more ammunition, 1,200 rounds, can be loaded. All this weight reduces the aircraft's speed and rate of climb but

it still has excellent range with flight duration of up to two and a half hours.

And when there don't seem to be many enemy tanks around but plenty of soldiers, the Hellfires are left in their crates and double loads of the Hydra 70mm rockets carried instead along with the full bin of 1,200 rounds of 30mm ammunition for the Area Weapons System; thus prepared the Apaches are ready to swoop down on the opposing force just like their namesakes.

The weapons are only one part of the story. Apaches are designed to take hits as well as deliver them, and both the crew and critical aircraft components are protected by armor against 23mm rounds and similar hazards, and the crew seats absorb some of the shock of impact during a crash, both features Army aviators of the old school would have appreciated.

Sensor systems in the nose provide the crew with images of the terrain ahead and to the sides, for targeting and for navigation, day or night, fair weather or foul. The CPG (co-pilot/gunner) sits in the forward seat and uses controls and sight systems similar in function to those used by Abrams and Bradley gunners. A laser rangefinder/designator calculates the range to targets and marks them for engagement. Included are a daylight television system, a forward-looking infra-red (FLIR) target acquisition and designation system (TADS), and a color video system. The

RIGHT: *Apache pilots use a unique helmet with some special features. On the bulkhead behind his seat, sensors monitor the head position of this pilot; they are sensitive enough that he can provide targeting data to the aircraft's fire control system by looking at an object through the monocle in front of his right eye and pressing a switch on one of the flight controls.*

FAR RIGHT: *An Apache can operate at high altitudes, but seldom fights from there. Like its namesake, the modern Apache warrior is at home out in the weeds, peeking around rocks and trees, and taking its adversaries by surprise,*

NEXT PAGE: *"Gremlin Six" -- Rick Rife (a captain at the time this photo was made, a colonel now).*

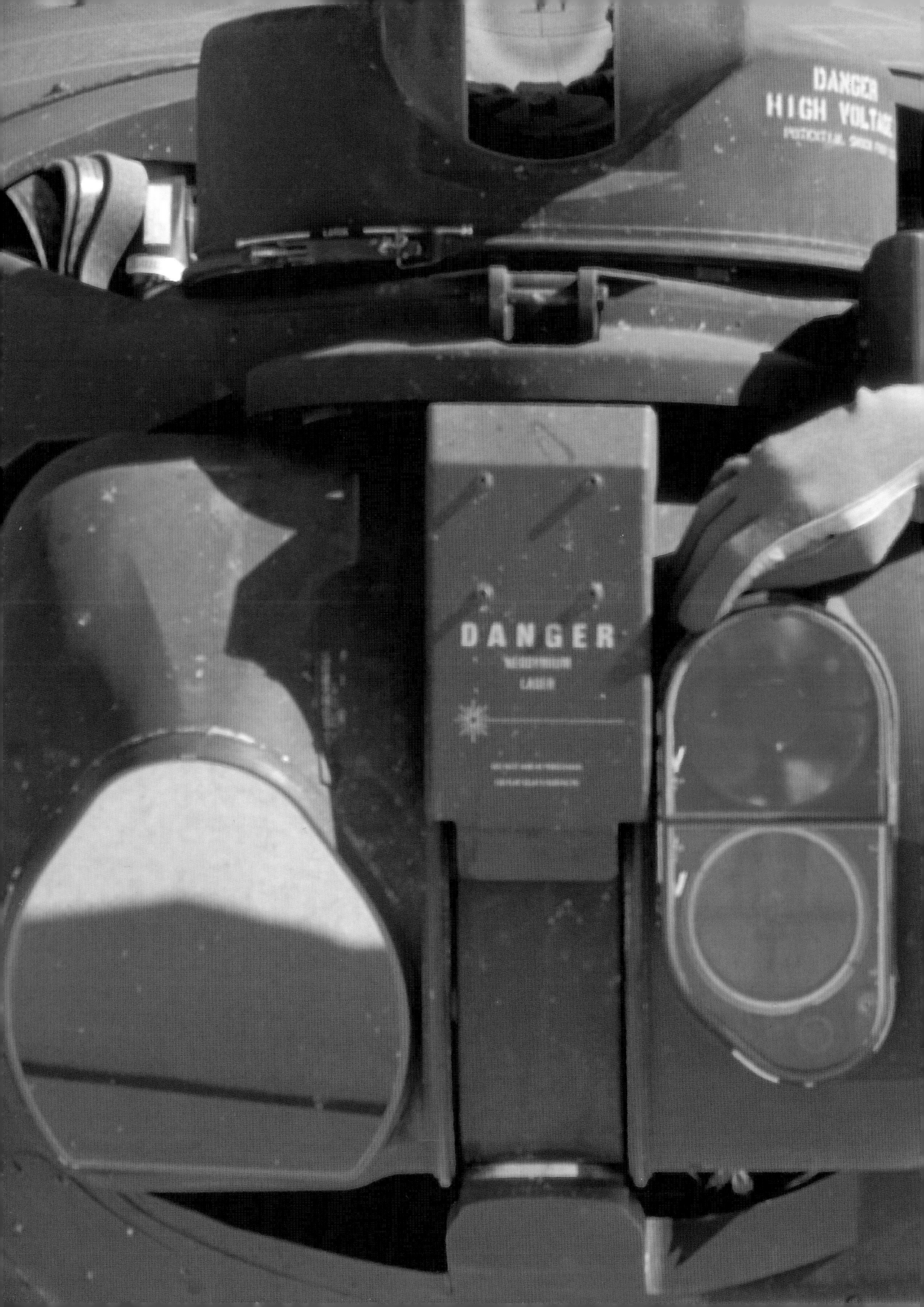
DANGER
HIGH VOLTAG
DANGER
LASER

LEFT: *A brace of 70mm free-flight rockets depart downrange. Although not precision weapons, rockets have been extremely useful over the years and Army helicopters have been firing them in combat since at least 1963.*

INSET, RIGHT: *The Longbow version of the AH-64 is easily identified by its sensor housing above the rotor head.*

INSET, LEFT: *The monocle is a kind of minature version of the fighter pilot's HUD, or Head Up Display, complete with basic flight data (altitude, speed, direction of travel) and weapons system information that is visible regardless of where he is looking.*

PREVIOUS PAGE: *Apaches can take out tanks, trucks, bunkers, troops in the open, aircraft on the ground, enemy convoys, and a wide variety of other targets, day or night, rain or shine.*

Attack helicopters have evolved tremendously in the past few years, with many features to enhance crew survivability and mission performance. Engine exhaust is dispersed upward into the rotorwash, helping to defeat heat-seeking missiles. Both seats are designed to absorb impact forces in a crash and armor protects pilots and critical aircraft components from small arms fire and some larger weapons.

TADS/FLIR provides stabilized images at normal and high magnifications, and also allows the gunner to track a moving target automatically by "boxing" it in the sight. The system will then track the target, maintaining a firing solution on it, until the gunner or pilot decides to engage.

UH-60 Black Hawk

Black Hawk helicopters are the Ford F-150 pickup trucks of the Army, highly popular, used for everything, reliable, and economical. The Black Hawk is the descendant of the battle-tested UH-1 Huey, but far more powerful and commodious. Its twin gas turbine engines provide safety along with the torque to pull a moose through a kazoo—or lift M119 howitzers, their crews, and enough ammunition to fire an artillery raid. You can get a whole squad of eleven smelly, filthy, bloody Rangers or infantrymen in one of them, and haul them out of a hot LZ, day or night, rain or shine. The UH-1 was good for about half that load, daylight only, reasonably fair weather only.

You haven't lived till you've ridden a Black Hawk on a night assault in mountainous terrain on a moonless night when it is blacker than the inside of a cow. Both pilots use their "NODS" or night vision devices to see the terrain, but for those in back, it is a roller coaster ride in the dark because, day or night, Army aviation sticks close to the ground. This kind of flight is called NOE or "nap of the earth," and uses terrain masking to keep hostile eyes and ears from tracking the flight's progress. Down low, the noise of the helicopter's blades is absorbed and dissipated far better than when the helicopter is flying above the terrain.

If you happen to be a door gunner, manning an M60 on a flex mount on either side of the fuselage, all that is really visible is the dim outline of hills, ridges, and treelines as they roar past just a few feet under the aircraft. Small flashes of static electricity flicker from the blade tips. Inside, the Black Hawk's cargo of infantry soldiers clutch their weapons and endure the ride, praying for it to be over soon—one way or another.

THIS PAGE: *UH-60 Black Hawk helicopters and their crews can be found all around the Army, giving people and their gear a lift in and out of some quite exotic locations. SPIE rigging will get you out of the jungle and sling-loads will deliver your artillery, ammunition, and crew. Excellent and reliable navigation systems allow pilots to get to the right spot under any conditions – but they consult the map anyway.*

NEXT PAGE: *Black Hawks will handle extremely heavy loads like this pair of 105mm howitzers.*

NEXT PAGE, INSET: *"Wait for me!" A member of an artillery gun crew dashes for his ride home, a Black Hawk already light on the gear and anxious to "pull pitch" and get the hell out of Dodge.*

CH-47 Chinook

The Army's workhorse medium cargo helicopter has been carrying troops, artillery, vehicles, and bulky gear for more than forty years when it helped pioneer the airmobility concept at Fort Benning and the experimental 11th Air Assault Division. The early ones were rated to carry up to 10,000 pounds under ideal conditions; today's Delta models are good for up to 26,000 pounds. They've been absorbing more bullet holes in Afghanistan where their high-altitude capability has helped the soldiers go places and do things faster, safer, more effectively than could be done with any other combat vehicle or aircraft.

As with other Army helicopters, there are many variations on the basic airframe. Some are designed for special operations, with inflight refueling probes, extra communications systems, armor, and weapons mounts. The spec sheet will tell you the Chinook can carry up to forty four combat equipped troopers, but that's mostly wishful thinking. Three external hooks permit the CH-47 to carry vehicles, cannon, fuel bladders, pallets of ammunition and barrier materials, and anything else weighing less than thirteen tons out in the breeze. There's even one called the Fat Cow whose mission is to refuel other helicopters at remote FARPs (Forward Arm and Refuel Points), especially handy for those deep penetration raids.

Australian infantry on a joint exercise with US Army personnel disembark from a CH47 , one of the first cargo helicopters to be designed around gas turbine, instead of reciprocating, engine technology. The Chinook has been in the Army inventory for forty years, and some aircraft still flying have been in service that long, although rebuilt entirely. The bullet holes, carefully patched, can still be discovered on many of them, though – mute testimony to adventures in the combat zone. These aircraft, from the California National Guard, routinely perform rescue missions as well as conventional military chores.

OH-58 Kiowa

Superficially resembling the civilian Bell Jet Ranger helicopter from which its airframe and drive-train was derived, the OH-58 Kiowa is another old Viet Nam era design that has been adapted for modern battles. The Kiowa is an armed scout, able to sneak and peek around ridges and tree-lines, watch what the enemy is doing, report back, designate targets, and even engage targets on its own.

Until the D, or "Delta" model, came along, the OH-58 was a pretty simple machine with a pretty simple mission. But the addition of the Mast Mounted Sight – commonly called the "million-dollar beach ball" – and a set of improved radios and navigation tools made this old warrior more important than ever. Inside the MMS is a vibration-stabilized video camera with a very long reach and the ability to use thermal as well as visible light sensors. The camera allows the pilot and enlisted observer to watch enemy behavior far beyond the range of the "Mk One Eyeball." While they are watching, only the "beachball" needs to be exposed to enemy view as the pilot hovers behind trees or rocks. A laser designator can mark targets to be serviced by tube artillery and 155mm Copperhead projectiles. The same designator can provide targeting data for AH-64 Apaches or Air Force "fast-movers."

But one of the features that has made the old Kiowa especially valuable today is the addition of its own suite of weapons: two Hellfire missiles, pods of 70mm Hydra free-flight rockets, a fixed .50cal heavy machine gun, and the most exciting development of all, air-to-air Stinger missiles. The Stingers finally give the Army a way to fight enemy helicopters effectively – a major heartburn in the past.

Kiowas have been scouting for the Army for many years, a design based on the Bell Jet Ranger and adapted for military use. Stuffed with radios and nav gear, they are superb at recon missions, prowling the distant edges of the battlefield.

Reference

CURRENT
US ARMY—Official US Army Site
www.goarmy.com

Recruiting information about full-time and part-time job opportunities.

The United States Army Homepage
www.army.mil/

News, career information, publications, photographs, and links to other Army and Department of Defense pages.

Association of the United States Army
www.ausa.org/

Homepage of the Association of the United States Army — the voice for the Army.

Army Research Office
www.aro.army.mil/

The Army Research Office "empowers the Army with Science." There are many interesting documents and subjects for study.

Armylink
www.dtic.mil/armylink/

The official web site Office of the US Army Chief of Public Affairs.

US Army Corps of Engineers
www.usace.army.mil/

Homepage of the US Army Corps of Engineers—the world's premier public engineering organization.

Army Publishing Directorate (APD)
www.usapa.army.mil/

Home Page of the APD with information and ordering facilities on its publications. "The Army Publishing Directorate is the Army's leader in publishing and distributing information products, employing advanced technologies to ensure responsive support worldwide. Our primary mission is supplying official authenticated information to enhance the readiness of the total force."

United States Army Europe (USAREUR)
www.hqusareur.army.mil/

This is the homepage of USAREUR and Seventh Army, headquartered in Bamberg, Germany, with news and information for servcing personnel and members of trhe public.

HISTORY
Center of Military History
www.army.mil/cmh-pg/Books

Mass of information and links on the U.S. Army's history. Includes www.army.mil/cmh-pg/moh1.htm — a site dedicated to recording all of the Congressional Medal of Honor winners from the Civil War to the present. The citation for each winner is available.

US Army Military History Institute
carlisle-www.army.mil/usamhi/

The US Army Military History Institute provides searchable databases of bibliographical and biographical holdings and unit histories, photographs, maps and other material. Its intent is to "preserve the Army's History and ensure access to historical research materials."

US ARMY Insignia
www2.powercom.net/~rokats/army-home.html

History and illustrations of Army insignia, rank badges and medals.

Hyperwar US Army in World War II
www.ibiblio.org/hyperwar/USA/index.html

Part of the mammoth Hyperwar US Army in World War II project, this site has a wealth of publications, research material and information for the student or historian.

Grunts.net
www.grunts.net/

"The home of military history." This page provides first-hand accounts and photographs with more considered pieces on U.S. military history. Includes sections on African-Americans in the US military.

Globalsecurity.org
www.globalsecurity.org/

Whoever is running this Global Security organization should be commended for crispness and its attention to many facets of U.S. history, as well as its up-to-date features.

MUSEUMS & REENACTMENT
Military Museums
usmilitary.about.com/cs/museums/

Excellent links to Army, Navy, Air Force, Coast Guard and other military museums.

Patton Museum of Cavalry and Armor
knox-www.army.mil/museum/gspatton.htm

The museum "displays German and Japanese war artifacts; an extensive collection of U.S. and foreign tanks and weaponry; and mementos of Patton's military career."

National Infantry Museum
www.benningmwr.com/museum.cfm

Set up in 1959 "to honor the infantry-man and his more than two centuries of proud service to the nation."

1st Division Museum at Cantigny
www.rrmtf.org/firstdivision/

Established in 1957 with the principal mission of promoting the history of the Big Red One.

82nd Airborne & Special Operations Museum Foundation
www.asomf.org/

A brand new and very impressive museum sited just outside Fort Bragg in Fayetteville itself.

JFK Special Warfare Museum Fort Bragg, North Carolina.

The JFK focuses on special operations from WWII to the present.

Thedropzone.org
www.thedropzone.org/misc/mission.html
On-line virtual museum of airborne subjects.

Normandyallies.org
www.normandyallies.org/index.htm

Organisation to remember and teach about the US side of D-Day, includes histories of units.

Reenactor.net
www.reenactor.net/main_htmls/ww2.html

Reenactor.net provides links to a wide variety of WWII reenacting including 2nd Armored.

355 HAL
Halberstadt, Hans.
Army